The Wonder of Grace

Herman Hoeksema

Reformed Free Publishing Association
Grand Rapids, Michigan
(Distributed by Kregel Publications)

Library of Congress Card Number:
81-85197

ISBN 0-916206-26-2

PRINTED IN THE UNITED STATES OF AMERICA

EDITOR'S PREFACE

This is the second edition of this little volume on the subject of salvation by grace only. Originally this work was published in 1944 by the Wm. B. Eerdmans Publishing Company. Its chapters were first a series of radio messages. Only some rather minor editorial changes and a few changes in format have been made in this new edition.

As we send forth this reprint, we repeat the wish of the author in his preface to the first edition: "May the God of our salvation so use the contents of the following pages that they who know and confess the truth of sovereign grace may be comforted and strengthened, the doubtful and hesitant may be established, those who preach a Christ that is impotent to overcome the perverse will of the sinner may be ashamed and converted, and, above all, God Who is really GOD may be glorified!"

— Homer C. Hoeksema

CONTENTS

I sought the Lord, and afterward I knew
He moved my soul to seek Him, seeking me;
It was not I that found, O Savior true;
No, I was found of Thee.
It was not I that found, O Savior true;
No, I was found of Thee, of Thee.

Thou didst reach forth Thy hand and mine enfold;
I walked and sank not on the storm-vexed sea;
'Twas not so much that I on Thee took hold,
As Thou, dear Lord, on me.
'Twas not so much that I on Thee took hold,
As Thou, dear Lord, on me, on me.

I find, I walk, I love; but O the whole
Of love is but my answer, Lord, to Thee!
For Thou wert long beforehand with my soul;
Always Thou lovedst me,
For Thou wert long beforehand with my soul;
Always, always, Thou lovedst me.

Chapter 1

THE IDEA OF SALVATION BY GRACE

> For by grace are ye saved.
> —Ephesians 2:8

The subject of which various aspects are discussed in the following pages should need no introduction to the believers in our Lord Jesus Christ. That we are saved by grace, not by works, and that, therefore, salvation is the work of God, in no wise of man, is a truth that touches upon the very heart of the gospel. "For by grace are ye saved, through faith; and that not of yourselves: it is the gift of God." (Ephesians 2:8) The doctrine of salvation by grace is one of those fundamental truths of the Christian faith of which the true knowledge and correct understanding are of great importance for the church of Christ in the world and for the believer individually. One who errs on this point must needs have a wrong conception of all the rest of Christian doctrine and corrupt the truth concerning God and man, concerning sin and redemption, concerning Christ and the church. Moreover, it is a subject of great practical significance for the believer, one that never fails to arouse his interest. He realizes that it concerns his only comfort in life and death: either he is saved by grace only, or he must needs perish. Hence, he never grows weary of hearing the gospel of salvation by sovereign grace proclaimed and expounded unto him in all the riches of its implications. And as he grows in the knowledge of this truth, he will grow in the grace of the Lord Jesus.

Small wonder, then, that from the earliest period of the history of the New Testament church this subject occupied a central place of interest. It was the theme of millions of sermons. Many a volume was written to expound and defend this truth. It is the theme of thousands of hymns. Often it was the occasion of sharp controversy. Today one

9

may hear of salvation by grace in sermon and song, from the pulpit and on the air, literally every day. And if, perhaps, it might seem well-nigh impossible to say anything about so thoroughly exhausted a subject that has not been said hundreds of times before, we may comfort ourselves with the thought that it may at least be possible to recall some very old truths in connection with our subject which are either forgotten or denied in modern times.

Our subject is, of course, rich in meaning and presents several aspects. To say that we are saved by grace expresses the truth that salvation is of the Lord. This should be emphasized from the outset. For grace is of God, and God is free and sovereign. To be saved by grace, then, means that grace is the only source, the sole explanation, the ultimate reason and ground of our salvation, the efficient cause of all that is implied in the work of our redemption and deliverance from sin and death. We are saved by grace only, without the work or cooperation of man, or we are not saved by grace at all. Hence, one who would speak of salvation by grace, must understand that he is speaking of a divine work throughout.

But all the works of God are eternal. Hence, salvation by grace has its source in eternity, and one cannot properly treat the subject of grace without considering the fundamental truth of divine and sovereign election: we are chosen by grace. For God "hath blessed us with all spiritual blessings in heavenly places in Christ, according as he hath chosen us in him before the foundation of the world." (Ephesians 1: 3, 4) Grace is sovereign. It is divine and, therefore, eternal. From the inscrutable depths of eternity spring all the spiritual blessings that lift us from the dark depths of sin and death into the glory of eternal life: the blessings of atonement and reconciliation, of redemption and deliverance, of regeneration and calling, of justification and sanctification, of the forgiveness of sins and the adoption unto children of God, of preservation and perseverance, of the resurrection from the dead and the final glorification. All these blessings of salvation are of pure grace: for "it is not of him that willeth, nor of him that runneth, but of God that sheweth mercy." (Romans 9:16) And all these various aspects of salvation by grace demand our consideration.

However, we might do well, first of all, to consider the general question: what is salvation? This question is by no means superfluous.

For, on the one hand, on our answer to this question must needs depend our conception of the part grace has in our salvation; and, on the other hand, especially in modern times the truth concerning salvation is distorted and corrupted in more than one way.

Salvation is not the same as reformation, the improvement of man and of the world; it has nothing in common with the modern notion of the building of character. This modernistic conception recognizes, indeed, that man is not what he ought to be. There is something wrong with him and with the world he is making. Especially in our own times, now the whole imposing structure of human culture and civilization threatens to collapse, this is deeply felt. However, it is maintained that man is not inherently corrupt. He is fundamentally good. But he is in need of reform. We must apply ourselves to man's reformation, to the building of his character, as well as to the improvement of his environment. And in this noble effort we must take Jesus as our example and turn to His teachings, especially to the Sermon on the Mount, for our program of reformation. If man only learns to follow in His steps and to apply His teachings to all his life and relationships, he will be saved. He will then learn to acknowledge that, like Jesus, so he, too, is the son of God; that God is the loving Father of all, and all men are brethren. And thus he will become a good, peace-loving creature, capable of making of the present world a kindgom of God in which righteousness shall dwell. Needless to say, in such a view of salvation there is no room for grace. Salvation is the work of proud man, not of God. And it is quite superfluous to prove that this human philosophy has nothing in common with the Biblical gospel of salvation.

However, it is not only in modernistic circles that one meets with a perverted presentation of the truth of salvation. On the contrary, also they who ostensibly preach the gospel of Christ, but in the meantime present the matter of salvation as something that ultimately depends for its realization on the will of man, distort the doctrine of sovereign grace. Salvation, according to this view, is something like a present that is all prepared and that is freely and graciously offered, but which one may either refuse or accept. Or it is like a kind invitation to some party or banquet, with which one may either comply or politely decline. So the sinner is offered salvation, chiefly consisting in escape from hell and entrance into heaven after this life, on condition that he will accept Christ. This salvation is all prepared for the sinner. In himself he is damned, worthy of eternal death. But Christ died for every sinner, and merited for all the forgiveness of sins, righteousness, and eternal glory.

So far it is all of grace.

And that the gospel is preached to sinners and this glorious redemption is offered them freely, that, too, is of grace.

But it is at this point that salvation as a work of divine grace and power ends. For beyond the merited redemption of Christ and the offered salvation, grace is not sovereign and efficacious: it is powerless to save and actually to deliver from the dominion of sin and death, except by the sinner's consent. If the sinner only accepts the salvation that is offered to him, if only he will say, "I accept Christ as my personal Savior," all will be well with him, and grace can proceed; but if he is recalcitrant and stubbornly declines the earnest invitation to be saved, grace can do nothing with him. Many a preacher does not hesitate openly and boldly to declare that God is powerless to save the sinner unless the latter gives his consent, and that Christ can do no more than He did unless the sinner permits Him to proceed with His work of salvation. Jesus is willing to save, but His willingness must suffer shipwreck on the rock of man's contrary and refractory will. He stands at the door of the sinner's heart and knocks; but the key of the door is on the inside, and the Savior cannot enter, unless the sinner opens the door.

From this arises that very common form of preaching that is erroneously called evangelical and that always reaches its climax in the well-known, extremely sensational "altar call." I say *erroneously,* for "evangelical preaching" is preaching of the gospel; and the true gospel never presents a powerless God or a Christ impotent to save. Since the grace of God is dependent on the choice of the sinner's will, it follows that the persuasion of human language, of the voice of the preacher, pleading and begging, may assist him to make the right choice and induce him to let Jesus into his heart!

Thus Christ is travestied!

O, to be sure, salvation is deliverance from hell and damnation. "He that believeth on the Son hath everlasting life, but he that believeth not the Son shall not see life; but the wrath of God abideth on him." (John 3:36)

But, first of all, salvation is much more than the mere escape from punishment and hell and a check on the bank of heaven that is to be cashed after death. It is a wonderwork of the Almighty, Who quickeneth the dead and calleth the things that are not as if they were. (Romans 4:17) It is a work in which God becomes revealed unto us in "the exceeding greatness of his power to usward who believe, according to the working of his mighty power, which he wrought in Christ, when he raised him from the dead, and set him at his own right hand in heavenly places." (Ephesians 1:19, 20) It is a work no less divine, and even more glorious, than the work of creation. All that is required to make of the sinner, dead in sin, filled with enmity against God, cursing the Almighty and raising his rebellious fist in the face of the Lord of heaven and earth, walking in darkness and hating the light — to make of such a sinner a righteous and holy child of God, humbly asking what God wills that he shall do, filled with the love of God, and for ever singing His praises, and to place that sinner, thus redeemed and delivered, in living fellowship with the glorious company of all the redeemed and glorified sinners, so that they together constitute a church, a beautiful house of God, a holy temple in the Lord, to the praise of the glory of His grace in the beloved — all this belongs to the work, the mighty work of God that is called salvation!

Secondly, salvation by grace means that it is an exclusively divine work, absolutely free and sovereign, in which man has no part at all and which does not in any sense depend upon the choice of man's will. Even as the work of creation is of God alone, which He accomplished without the cooperation of the creature, so the work of salvation is exclusively God's work, in which man has no part whatever. Even as Adam lived and was an active creature, not in or before his being created, but by virture of this marvelous work of God, so the sinner lives, and becomes positively active, so that he wills to be saved and embraces Christ, not in cooperation with God Who saves him but as a result of the wonder of grace performed upon him. Salvation by grace implies that grace is always first. True, "whosoever will may come," but the will to come is not prevenient to grace but subsequent to it as its fruit.

Consider from what depths of darkness and death salvation delivers man and unto what heights of life and glory it exalts him, and judge for yourselves whether at any particular stage of this marvelous work of

God man could be a cooperating party with God. Popularly, salvation has often been defined as that wonderwork of God whereby He delivers the sinner from the greatest evil and makes him partaker of the highest good. But what is the greatest evil from which grace delivers the sinner? Listen to the words of Scripture in Ephesians 2:1-3: "And you...who were dead in trespasses and sins; wherein in times past ye walked according to the course of this world, according to the prince of the power of the air, the spirit that now worketh in the children of disobedience: Among whom also we all had our conversation in times past in the lust of our flesh, fulfilling the desires of the flesh and of the mind; and were by nature the children of wrath, even as others." That is the evil from which grace saves us!

And what does it mean that, apart from grace, we are dead in trespasses and sins?

O, it signifies exactly what it says: that by our sins we are, by nature, just as dead unto God and righteousness, unto all good works, as the corpse in the grave is dead unto all activity of any kind. It means that, apart from grace, we are wholly incapable of doing any good, or even of thinking and willing anything that is pleasing to God. We are bound from within with unbreakable shackles of darkness and corruption. We are slaves of sin, willing slaves to be sure, but slaves withal, loving darkness rather than the light. And this spiritual, ethical death is God's own wrath upon us: the punishment for sin. For we are children of wrath from our birth, guilty and damnable because of Adam's transgression. And we can only daily increase our guilt and our damnation.

Such is our miserable plight! There is a debt we can never pay, nor do we care to pay it. There is a power of corruption from which we cannot and will not deliver ourselves. There is wrath and damnation from which we can never escape, nor do we care to, or seek to escape: for we are enemies of God, and the carnal mind is death!

In that horrible depth of misery grace finds the sinner.

Do you imagine, then, that he is capable or willing to cooperate with God to his own salvation, or that any emotional and sentimental plea of a preacher will persuade him to desire to seek salvation in Christ? I tell you *Nay*. Before grace takes hold of that sinner and raises him from the dead, he will always refuse to accept the proffered salvation and will prefer death to life, sin to righteousness, the devil to God! He must be saved by grace as a divine wonder!

Consider, too, unto what heights of glory grace saves the sinner. He is made partaker of the highest good! But what is the highest good? It is eternal life! Yes, but what is eternal life? Is it a sort of carnally conceived everlasting state of bliss in a beautiful place called heaven? God forbid! O, to be sure, heaven is blessed and beautiful. But it is so principally because God is there, and Christ is there, and the saints in Christ are there. And the blessedness of heaven consists in this, that it is the house of God, and that in that house we may dwell in fellowship with the living God, a fellowship that is more intimate than the first man Adam ever tasted: for it has its center in the incarnated Word of God, our Lord Jesus Christ! To be the perfect sons of God, knowing God even as we are known, righteous as He is righteous, holy as He is holy, loving and beloved forever, seeing Him face to face, and having our delight in the doing of His will and the keeping of His precepts, loving Him with all our heart and mind and soul and strength in heavenly perfection and glory — that is the blessedness of heaven, and that is the height of glory to which grace raises us in Jesus Christ our Lord! But do you imagine that there could be any cooperation on the part of that miserable sinner we just described to reach that height of perfection? Or would you say that the sinner who is an enemy of God even longs for that perfect fellowship with God, that he who loves darkness is capable of yearning for that state of perfect and everlasting light? I tell you *Nay*. He is saved by grace, and by grace only, as a wonderwork of Him Who raises the dead and calleth the things that are not as if they were!

Saved by grace! Delivered from wrath, guilt, damnation, corruption, and death — all by grace! Clothed with righteousness, holiness, life, and glory — by grace only! Translated into light, from death into life, from shame into glory, from hell into heaven — all by the power of God's wondrous grace! And all because of the eternal, sovereign love of Him Who chose the things that are not to bring to nought the things that are; that no flesh should glory in His presence!

Chapter 2

CHOSEN BY GRACE

> According as he hath chosen
> us in him before the foundation of
> the world.
>
> — Ephesians 1:4

In the previous chapter we remarked that, even though it might be well-nigh impossible to bring out some new truths in respect to so old a subject as that of salvation by grace, one might at least wipe the dust of oblivion from some very old and fundamental aspects of this doctrine and give new emphasis to some truths which in our day are either denied or forgotten.

One of these truths is the Biblical doctrine of sovereign election unto salvation. This is surely not a popular doctrine. Especially in our day, it does not meet with universal favor, even among those who profess to believe that a sinner is saved by grace only. That sovereign grace must needs be particular grace, and that particular grace presupposes free and sovereign election, is a truth which by many is looked upon as belonging in the ecclesiastical or dogmatical antique shop. Much more popular are they in our day who openly and boldly deny the doctrine of God's sovereign predestination and who preach salvation as a possibility, a chance for all. God on His part seriously seeks the salvation of all men, and He offers it to all. And man has the power by an act of his own free will either to accept or to reject the proffered salvation. There can be no doubt that, if the truth were to be determined by popular vote, the doctrine of sovereign election would be rejected by an overwhelming majority.

However, this is no reflection on the doctrine of election. The truth has never been popular; and a majority vote surely cannot be trusted to

17

determine what is the truth concerning God, Christ, man, and his salvation. For this we must always turn to the Word of God itself. And if we accept unconditionally the teachings of Holy Scripture, there can be no doubt in our minds that God has sovereignly chosen such as shall be saved. Our Savior, reviewing the fruits of His labors in Galilee, utters this remarkable thanksgiving to the Father: "I thank thee, O Father, Lord of heaven and earth, because thou hast hid these things from the wise and prudent, and revealed them unto babes. Even so, Father: for so it seemed good in thy sight. All things are delivered unto me of my Father: and no man knoweth the Son but the Father; neither knoweth any man the Father, save the Son, and he to whomsoever the Son will reveal him." (Matthew 11:25-27) To the Jews in Capernaum who reject Him the Lord proclaims triumphantly: "All that the Father giveth me shall come to me." And again: "No man can come to me, except the Father which hath sent me draw him." (John 6:37, 44) When the Jews in Jerusalem believe not on Him, the Savior explains that this is because they are not of His sheep. His sheep hear His voice, and He knows them, and they follow Him; and He gives unto them eternal life; and no one shall ever pluck them out of His hand. And these sheep are those whom the Father gave Him, for thus the Lord explains: "My Father which gave them me is greater than all, and no man can pluck them out of my Father's hand." (John 10:26-29) In Romans 8:28 we are assured that all things work together for good to them that love God. And why? Because they that love God are the called according to God's eternal purpose. And what is this eternal purpose? This: "For whom he did foreknow, he also did predestinate to be conformed to the image of his Son, that he might be the first-born among many brethren. Moreover whom he did predestinate, them he also called: and whom he called, them he also justified: and whom he justified, them he also glorified." (Romans 8:29, 30) To Rebecca it was said: "The elder shall serve the younger," and that, too, before the children were born, and had done either good or evil, "that the purpose of God according to election might stand, not of works, but of him that calleth. . . . As it is written, Jacob have I loved, but Esau have I hated." (Romans 9:11-13) "For he saith to Moses, I will have mercy on whom I will have mercy, and I will have compassion on whom I will have compassion. So then it is not of him that willeth, nor of him that runneth, but of God that sheweth mercy." (Romans 9:15, 16) And the God and Father of our Lord Jesus Christ "hath blessed us with all spiritual blessings in heavenly places in Christ: according as he hath chosen us in him before the foundation of the world." (Ephesians 1:3, 4) And he has "predestinated us unto the adoption of children by Jesus Christ unto himself, according to the good pleasure of his will." (Ephesians 1:5) And in Christ "we have obtained an inheritance, being predestinated according to the purpose of him who worketh all things after the counsel of his own will." (Ephesians 1:11) Much more might be quoted, but this should suffice to prove that the doctrine of election unto salvation is quite Scriptural.

It is, of course, quite impossible in these pages to explain this doctrine in all its implications. Let me briefly state, in the first place, that the Scriptural doctrine of election means that God has from all eternity sovereignly determined who shall be saved in Christ Jesus, ordained all the ways and means unto their salvation, and that, too, in distinction from others whom He purposed not to save. And we will have to mark especially three elements of this truth: it is a *personal* election, it is *sovereign* election, and it is *organic* election.

It is *personal* election. By this is meant that it is an election of persons, whose names God has written from all eternity in the book of life. We emphasize this over against the view of those who try to explain the Scriptural teaching concerning election as if it only meant that God chose a nation, the nation of Israel, and that, too, not unto eternal salvation, but unto some temporal, national privileges; or of those who explain that God chose really certain conditions, such as faith in Christ, and, therefore, may be said to have elected believers unto eternal life. Jacob and Esau appear very much as persons in Romans 9:13. And we read that when Paul preached the gospel to the Gentiles in Antioch in Pisidia "as many as were ordained to eternal life believed." (Acts 13:48)

Secondly, we must emphasize that election is absolutely sovereign. By this we mean that God is the Lord also of salvation, and that the ground and motive of His choosing some unto salvation must not be sought in man, but in God alone. Election is of grace, not of works. It is necessary to mark this with special emphasis over against those who seek the ground of their election in the elect themselves. Granted,

they say, that Scripture teaches personal predestination, so that God
from all eternity ordained who should be saved, this cannot possibly
imply that in His election God had no regard for the character and
works of the elect. He chose the best. The ultimate ground of election
and reprobation cannot be the mere sovereign pleasure of the Most
High. That would be arbitrary. It would present God as a willful
tyrant. Hence, predestination rests on God's foreknowledge. It is
based on foreseen good works. God foresaw and foreknew from all
eternity who would be willing to believe and to accept Christ and who
would reject Him, and election means that He ordained the former unto
eternal life and glory. Election, then, is not sovereign. It is contingent
upon the will of man. It is not of grace, but of works. For the Bible
teaches that whosoever will may take of the water of life freely. But
this is not according to the Word of God. To be sure, we have no
objection to the gospel that whosoever will may come and take of the
water of life freely. And we may add that all who come will surely be
received: for their very will to come is already the fruit of grace and
the outflow of eternal election. For faith or the will to believe is not
the ground of God's election; but, on the contrary, man's will to come
to Christ is the fruit of God's predestinating grace. For it is not of him
that willeth, nor of him that runneth, but of God that sheweth mercy.
(Romans 9:16) And of the Gentiles in Antioch it is not said that as
many of them as believed, or were willing to believe, were ordained to
life; but, on the contrary, as many as were ordained to eternal life
believed. We are not chosen because we were better than others, for
like them we are children of wrath by nature. There is absolutely
nothing to boast. Election is sovereign. It rests in God alone. It is of
grace. God is the Lord!

But election is also *organic*. When we insist, on the basis of Scripture, that election is personal, we do not mean that God arbitrarily
determined to save a number of persons, and just as arbitrarily let the
rest go to perdition. There is no arbitrariness with God. All His works
in time and eternity are perfect, and characterized by highest wisdom.
Election is according to His eternal purpose. And that purpose is the
highest revelation of the glory of God, through Jesus Christ, the incarnated Son of God, the firstborn of every creature, Who died and rose
again, and Who is exalted at the right hand of God; and out of Jesus

Christ, that glory of God must be manifested through the millions upon millions of glorified elect who will know Him and declare His glorious praises, and through all the new creation, the new heavens and the new earth in which righteousness shall dwell. To that grand purpose election is subservient. By that purpose it is dominated. Hence, God did not choose an arbitrary number of people; He chose a church, the body of Christ, a holy temple in the Lord. Now a temple is not a mere pile of bricks and other building material, the larger the better: it is a beautiful whole, representing an idea, in which each part must occupy its own place in order to serve the beauty of the whole, so that the number as well as the position of each part is determined by the whole. The same is true of the church. It is one grand whole, representing one idea, the glory of God in Christ, conceived by the perfect artificer; and the position but also the number of all the members of that whole is determined in the eternal wisdom and purpose of Him Who worketh all things according to the counsel of His own will. And presently, when all the elect shall have been gathered, and the church of all ages shall have been perfected and glorified, it shall stand at the head of the new creation, in which all things shall be united in Christ, and God shall be all in all! That is election!

This doctrine is of fundamental importance and of great practical significance.

Quite properly, it has been called the *cor ecclesiae,* the heart of the church. The whole system of the doctrine of salvation by grace is built on it as its foundation, stands or falls with this truth. If you deny or distort this basic truth, you may, perhaps, inconsistently continue to speak of salvation by grace for a time, but ultimately you will surely lose all the great doctrines of salvation. Deny it, and you cannot maintain the truth of total depravity: for if to some extent you present salvation as contingent upon the will and choice of the sinner, you must ascribe to him some remnant of goodness in virtue of which he is able to make the right determination and choice. Refuse to accept the doctrine of sovereign election, and you must ultimately deny the truth of vicarious atonement. For if Christ's death is substitutional, those for whom He died are certainly justified and reconciled to God. But it is evident that all men are not saved. Hence, you must choose between two alternatives: Christ represented the elect, or in His death He did not really pay for the sins of those for whom He died. Election and vicarious atonement are inseparably connected. The same is true of the relation of election and all the blessings of salvation which are bestowed on us in Christ Jesus our Lord, of calling and faith, of justification and sanctification, of hope and love, of preservation and perseverance. Either these are all blessings of grace, and then they flow from sovereign election; or they depend upon the will and work of man, and then they are not of grace. The doctrine of election is of central importance for the whole system of the truth of salvation.

But this truth is also of immense practical significance. It is the indispensable condition for all true religion. For all true religion is God-centered. And this is true only of that religion that has its ultimate source in God's sovereign election. For it alone confesses that God is all and that man is absolutely nothing. There remains nothing for man to boast. All his own goodness, good will, works, religion, piety are cast into the dust as having no value before God. For we are saved according as we are chosen. And we are chosen, not because we distinguished ourselves from others, not because of any goodness or willingness on our part, but solely because it pleased God to distinguish us, and only by grace. God is all! We bring nothing to Him, He gives all to us. We have nothing to boast. Let Him that glorieth glory in the Lord!

Besides, this doctrine affords us unspeakable consolation and is the source of all true comfort and assurance. It dare not be objected to this doctrine that this truth offers no comfort to poor sinners: for nothing could be farther from the truth. True, this doctrine has no consolation for the impenitent wicked. But we ask: is there any form of presentation of the gospel that could possibly comfort the wicked and ungodly? There is no peace, saith my God, for the wicked! But is there a more comforting gospel than that of God's gracious election for the penitent, the seeking soul, the hungry and thirsty, the weary and heavy laden? He may be assured that he will be received and be saved: for his penitence, seeking, hunger and thirst, are the fruit of electing grace. Moreover, when we look about us in the world, full of confusion and madness, of corruption and apostasy, is there any assurance anywhere, except in the truth of God's sovereign election, that His work shall not fail, that His church shall surely be gathered, and His kingdom shall be established and manifested in glory?

Salvation is of the Lord: it shall surely be accomplished even unto the end! Let all the powers of darkness rave and rage and rise up against the living God and His Anointed, we know that even their ravings and fury can only be subservient and conducive to the realization of God's sovereign purpose of salvation. The gates of all hell cannot overwhelm the church! Nothing can separate us from the love of God which is in Christ Jesus our Lord!

Chapter 3

RECONCILED BY GRACE

... be ye reconciled to God.
— II Corinthians 5:20

The first part of the marvelous work of salvation to which we now call your attention is that of reconciliation. That we are saved by grace means, first of all, that we are reconciled by grace. In the wondrous work of salvation God reveals Himself as the Reconciler, full of grace and truth, rich in lovingkindness and tender mercies.

Of reconciliation the Scriptures speak very frequently, not only indirectly in all those passages which refer to the atonement in the blood of Christ, but also directly, using the term itself. "For if, when we were enemies, we were reconciled to God by the death of his Son, much more, being reconciled, we shall be saved by his life." (Romans 5:10) Well known is the passage from II Corinthians 5:18-20: "And all things are of God, who hath reconciled us to himself by Jesus Christ, and hath given to us the ministry of reconciliation; To wit that God was in Christ reconciling the world unto himself, not imputing their trespasses unto them, and hath committed unto us the word of reconciliation. Now then, we are ambassadors for Christ, as though God did beseech you by us: we pray you in Christ's stead, be ye reconciled to God." In Colossians 1:20 we are told even that God, having made peace through the blood of His cross, purposes to reconcile all things unto Himself, whether they be things in earth, or things in heaven. And then the Word of God continues: "And you, that were sometime alienated in your mind by wicked works, yet now hath he reconciled." (verse 21) Reconciliation is closely related to atonement and satisfaction for sin, as is evident from such passages as Hebrews 2:17: "Wherefore in all things it behooved him to be made like unto his brethren, that he might be a merciful and faithful high priest in things pertaining to God, to make reconciliation for the sins of the people."

From these passages a few outstanding truths are evident at once.

First of all, it is everywhere emphasized that God is the Author of this reconciliation, and that, too, absolutely alone, without any cooperation on our part. It is He that reconciles. We reconcile ourselves to God in no sense of the word. Nor does Christ, Who is the Mediator of this work of God, reconcile us to God. God reconciles us to Himself. No more than we have any part in the work of creation, no more have we any part in the work of reconciliation. What is more, we did not only have no part whatever in this divine work; we did not even desire reconciliation, neither seek it. On the contrary, on our part we did all we could to frustrate God's plan of redemption. For we were reconciled when we were enemies! And never did this enmity against God reveal itself in more horrible form than at the very moment when God reconciled us unto Himself: it was when we killed His Son, and that, too, through that very deed, God reconciled us unto Himself! When we were enemies, He reconciled us unto Himself through the death of His Son, Whom we killed! Surely we are reconciled by God alone and through pure grace!

Secondly, let us notice that God reconciled us unto Himself, not Himself to us. It is not the reconciliation of two parties to each other, but of men to God. Often one can read or hear that Christ as the Mediator reconciled us to God, and God to us. But this is a serious error. Scripture never speaks of God's reconciliation to us, nor could He be reconciled. He is the Reconciler, full of a mighty, unquenchable love; and He reconciles us to Himself.

Thirdly, let us note that this reconcilation is presented as an accomplished fact. It is not something that must still take place, or that is constantly being realized: nineteen hundred years ago, on the cross of Jesus Christ our Lord, the work of reconciliation was finished once for all. Through faith, and by grace, we enter into the state of reconciliation with God; but the reconciliation itself is an accomplished fact: we *are* reconciled to God!

What then is meant by reconciliation? It is that work of God whereby His own beloved elect were translated from a state of enmity and estrangement and wrath into a state of eternal and unchangeable

favor and most intimate friendship, and that, too, by the removal of
the cause of the estrangement, namely, sin, and the establishment of
an eternal righteousness.

Let us analyze this idea of reconciliation.

First of all, reconciliation is the restoration of an existing relationship, whether of love, or friendship, partnership, or some other alliance.
The actual existence of such a relationship is presupposed in reconciliation. This is true among men. You do not reconcile strangers. There is
no bond between them; there never was; and, therefore, no bond
between them can be restored. One may speak of reconciling man and
wife, between whom exists the sacred bond of matrimony, when they
drifted apart for some reason; or of the reconciliation of friends that
are at variance for a time; or of the servant to his master, or the subject
to his king. Always a relation or bond of friendship and love is understood. The same is true of God's work of reconciliation. It presupposes the eternal covenant relation of love and friendship into which
God entered with His people, a relation that is rooted in His eternal
purpose of election. That covenant relation can never be destroyed for
the simple reason that it rests wholly in God. God loves His people
with an eternal, unchangeable love. He never ceases to love them. No
matter what they may do or become, He still loves them. Though their
sins be as scarlet, and though they be red as crimson, He loves them
still, and will restore them to His favor and fellowship. He may be
angry with His people in righteous wrath for a moment, but even in
His anger He loves them. He is like a husband that loves and remains
faithful to his wife, no matter how often she may play the adulteress;
or like the father who, no matter how grievously his son may sin
against him, still loves that son and will receive him whenever he may
return. If this were not so, how could God be the Reconciler? Reconciliation is an act of infinite love, of unlimited grace, of abundant
mercy. God loved His people when they were enemies. Reconciliation
presupposes the eternal covenant relation of God with His people that
rests in God, the I Am, the Faithful and True!

Secondly, reconciliation implies that the parties to be reconciled
are at variance through some fault on the part of either or of both
parties. The relationship is disturbed for a time. It cannot properly
function because something intervened that makes the exercise of

friendship and love impossible. There is separation. One of the parties
in the matrimonial covenant was unfaithful, committed adultery; the
son sinned against his father and lives in that sin; the friend offended
his friend. The same is true of the relationship between God and His
people. He created them in His image and took them into His blessed
covenant in Adam. For Adam was the friend of God, clothed with
righteousness, the object of God's favor. He knew his God and was
known of Him. He loved his God and was loved by Him. He walked
and talked with God and was blessed by Him. But in and through
Adam the whole human race, and with the human race God's own
elect, violated the covenant relationship. They sinned and became
guilty, the objects of God's righteous wrath, foolish and corrupt,
enemies of God. And as they are in their sin and death, they cannot be
and function as God's covenant friends. Because of sin they are
alienated, and they have forfeited the right to God's favor and love.
The covenant relationship has been violated and disturbed. God is
terribly angry with His people in their sin, and they are in themselves
worthy of death and damnation!

Thirdly, if the disrupted relationship of friendship and love is to be
restored, the cause of the disruption must be removed. Among men
this may take place through repentance and confession on the part of
the party that had offended, and by the promise on his part henceforth
to be faithful to the relationship that was violated, and through forgiveness on the part of the one that was offended. An adulterous wife
may return to her husband in heartfelt sorrow, and be received by him;
and if the woman gives proof of her repentance and renewed faithfulness, the reconciliation is accomplished. The prodigal son returns to
his father in dust and ashes, confesses his sin and unworthiness, and his
father restores him to his place in the home. But with God this is
different. He cannot deny Himself. He cannot permit His holy law to
be trampled under foot with impunity. He cannot simply forgive and
forget. If the sinner's relation to Him is to be restored, the cause of
the separation must actually be removed, so that it is no more. But
how can sin be removed? How can the guilt of sin be blotted out?
How can the guilty become righteous? How can the object of God's
wrath be restored to His favor? There is one, and only one way: that
of perfect satisfaction! The sinner must atone for his sin. And atonement for sin consists in perfectly satisfying the justice of God!

But of what does this atonement consist? What can so satisfy the justice of God that the sinner's guilt is blotted out and that he is declared righteous before God? Again, there is only one answer: the sinner must freely, voluntarily, motivated by the love of God and true sorrow for his sin, bear the punishment of sin, eternal death! Mark you well, he must not merely bear the punishment and suffer eternal death, he must do so willingly; the bearing of the punishment must be an act of all his soul, and mind, and will, and heart, and strength. The damned in hell also suffer eternal death, yet they can nevermore atone. They are passive in their suffering. But he that would satisfy the justice of God against sin must *sacrifice himself.* He must be so mightily moved by the love of God that he seeks hell in order that he may atone, and that he voluntarily lays himself on the altar of God's holy wrath. For God's demand upon man is that he love Him. And this demand never changes. Even though man has become the object of God's consuming wrath, he must still love Him. He, therefore, who can perform that act of love, whereby he willingly allows himself to be consumed for God's righteousness' sake, satisfies God's justice.

Now it is at once evident that the mere sinner can never do this. As far as he is concerned, the case is hopeless. No good works, supposing that he could perform them, will ever atone for his sin: for he is obliged to do them in the first place; and as no man can pay a back debt by paying his current bills, so man cannot atone by doing good works. But the case with the sinner is much worse. He is dead in sin. He cannot do any good before God. He stands in enmity against God, and his nature is so corrupt that he loves the darkness rather than light. He is not at all concerned about the righteousness of God. How then could he possibly bring the sacrifice that would atone for his sin? Even if he would, he could not possibly bear the punishment of eternal death, and finish it, so that he would live. But he will not seek God. He does not care to be reconciled with God. It is clear then that his case is hopeless, and that, if he must reconcile himself to God, he will never be restored to God's favor. Reconciliation cannot be of man; it must be of God. It cannot be by works; it must be by grace!

And this is exactly the wonder of reconciliation: God reconciled us unto Himself while we were yet sinners! God was in Christ reconciling the world unto Himself. Never change this truth into something different. Never say that Christ reconciled God to us, and us to God.

That would make of Christ a third party between God and us. And although it is certainly true that Christ in His human nature is the Mediator of God and man, this Mediator is entirely of God! Nay, He is God Himself, the Son of God, begotten of the Father eternally, Who is eternally in the Father's bosom, God of God in human flesh! In Him the strong arm of the God of our salvation reaches down into our death, in order to remove the cause of our estrangement from Him, and to restore and raise to a higher, heavenly, eternal level the covenant of friendship between Him and us.

That is the meaning of the cross: God reconciled us to Himself through the death of His Son! There God was reconciling the world unto Himself, not imputing their trespasses unto them. There God Himself, through His Son in the flesh, satisfied His own justice. The Son of God brought the sacrifice that was required to blot out the guilt of sin and to clothe us with an everlasting righteousness. He could do so, because He was the holy child Jesus, the Lamb without blemish, and the zeal of God's house consumed Him. He could and did willingly, from the motive of the love of God, descend into lowest hell, to suffer the punishment of sin, to bear the wrath of God to the very end. He stood in the place of judgment, and on Him all the vials of God's wrath against sin were poured out. And when He cried out, "It is finished!" He had completed His sacrifice, removed sin, obtained righteousness, a fact which God sealed when He raised Him from the dead. And He was able to bring this sacrifice as an atonement for the sin of all His people. For God had appointed Him to be the head of His church, representing them. For them He died. And, because it is not mere man, but the Son of God Who died on the cross, His death is abundantly sufficient to blot out the guilt of all His own!

And so the gospel is the ministry of reconciliation. It proclaims that reconciliation is an accomplished fact: the elect are surely reconciled to God. He reconciled us! We are reconciled by grace, by pure, free, sovereign grace! And it is He, too, Who sends out the word of reconciliation. For He gave unto the apostles the ministry of reconciliation, and put the very word of reconciliation in their very hearts, so that they had the power and authority to speak in the name of God the Reconciler, and so that they became ambassadors of Christ, as though God did beseech us by them: "Be ye reconciled to God!"

(II Corinthians 5:18-20) This word of reconciliation is still proclaimed among us, from the Scriptures, and through His own ministry of the Word by the preachers He Himself sends unto us.

Be ye reconciled to God!

That is God's own prayer! O, marvelous grace!

What is more, it is by His own grace that His own prayer is heard, and that the sinner turns to God the Reconciler. For He causes the word of reconciliation to become a mighty power within us, a fire in our bones, so that we repent of sin in dust and ashes and seek reconciliation with God in the blood of Christ!

It is all of Him, none of us!

Let him that glorieth glory in the Lord!

Chapter 4

UNITED WITH CHRIST BY GRACE

> For if we have been planted together in the likeness of his death, we shall be also in the likeness of his resurrection.
>
> — Romans 6:5

We are saved by grace not only in the sense that Christ merited all the blessings of salvation for us by His death and perfect obedience, so that we are reconciled to God, but also in this sense, that it is the power of grace which delivers us from all the power of sin and death and makes us actual partakers of righteousness and eternal life.

The word *grace* has different connotations in Scripture. It may refer merely to an attribute, a perception, a virtue of God: God is gracious in Himself, apart from any relation which He sustains toward us. Grace then means that God is beautiful in His perfections and that He is pleasant and attractive, as well as that He is eternally attracted by His own virtues. There are pleasures with our God for evermore. Grace may also denote a disposition and attitude of God towards the creature, and then it signifies favor. And when this favor is revealed to those who are themselves unworthy of it, who have forfeited it through sin, it stands in opposition to works. It is, of course, this aspect of grace which is revealed in salvation, particularly in God's justifying the ungodly in Christ, and thus reconciling us unto Himself. But this is not all. The term *grace* also is used in Scripture to denote that power and divine operation upon us and within us whereby we are actually delivered from the dominion of sin and death, whereby we are liberated from sin's slavery, changed from guilty children of darkness into righteous and living children of the light. Also this grace operates upon us from the God of our salvation through Jesus Christ our Lord. Christ is not only the Mediator of our redemption; He is also the Mediator of our deliverance. From Him we receive all the spiritual blessings of salvation. And in order to receive them, we must be united with Christ, incorporated in Him, become one plant with Him. It is to this incorporation into Christ, this spiritual union with Him, that we must now call your attention.

The first truth which we must somewhat understand in this connection is that Christ *is* our salvation, and that all the spiritual blessings of salvation which we need to become and to remain children of God, redeemed, delivered, sanctified, and glorified, are in Him. This truth is frequently expressed in the Word of God. The apostle Paul writes in I Corinthians 1:30 that Christ Jesus "is made unto us wisdom, and righteousness, and sanctification, and redemption." In Ephesians 2:14 he writes that Christ *is* our peace. *In* Him we have redemption through His blood, the forgiveness of sins, according to Colossians 1:14; and in chapter 2:3 of the same epistle we are told that in Him are hid all the treasures of wisdom and knowledge. For it pleased the Father that in Him all fulness should dwell, and in Him does dwell all the fulness of the Godhead bodily. (Colossians 1:19; 2:9) Our Lord Himself proclaims that He is the bread of life, so that if anyone cometh unto Him, he shall never hunger (John 6:35, 48); that He is the living bread, which, if any man eat, he shall live forever (John 6:51); and He presents Himself as the water of life, and calls the thirsty to Him that they may drink. He *is* the light of the world; and he that follows after Him shall have the light of life. (John 8:12) He *is* the resurrection and the life; and he that believeth in Him shall never die. (John 11:25, 26) He *is* the way, the truth, and the life. (John 14:6)

Let us try to understand the implication of this as clearly as possible. For it is exactly in this respect that no man ever spake, nor will any man ever be able to speak as our Savior. And it is because of these claims of Christ that men marveled at Him, but also were offended in Him. You never heard a man speak thus, did you? Nor did you ever hear of a man or read about a mere man that spake thus. Philosophers may probably tell you how you may find life and happiness and satisfaction, and how the world may find rest and peace; and even so, their philosophy always fails and disappoints those who put their trust in it.

But this man said boldly and absolutely: "I *am* the resurrection and the life! I *am* the bread of life! I *am* the fountain of living water! I *am* the light of the world! I *am* the way, the truth, the life!" He called men unto Him not in order to instruct them as to the best way to happiness; but He boldly promised that He would *give* them life, rest, peace, everlasting satisfaction. And so He *is* our righteousness, wisdom and knowledge, peace and rest, sanctification and redemption. He *is* our all. All the spiritual blessings of salvation which we need to translate us from death into life, from darkness into light, from corruption into righteousness, and to raise us from lowest hell to highest heaven, are in Him. For He did not only die that He might be our righteousness in a juridical sense; He also arose, and He also was exalted at the right hand of God, and He also received the Spirit without measure, in order that as the quickening Spirit He might set us free and bestow upon us the grace of eternal life.

We might, perhaps, employ a few simple illustrations to elucidate the meaning of all this. You all know that in our towns and villages we receive the water in our homes from a central reservoir, or tank or water tower, into which it is pumped from some natural source in the first place. Or, to use another illustration, you are acquainted with the fact that the electric current which brings light into your home is generated in some central power plant in the city in which you live. And the gas which you use to cook your food or to heat your home reaches you from huge storage tanks. From the one reservoir all the homes in your city are supplied with drinking water. That one power plant generates all the electricity used in your town and illuminates all your homes. From the one central gas plant flows the gas which supplies the whole city. Well, so Christ is the spiritual power-plant in the entire New Jerusalem, from Whom the current of life and light flows into your soul. He is the one and only central storage tank in the entire kingdom of God, the sole reservoir, out of which flows continually all the water of life to quench the thirst of all the citizens of that kingdom. He is God's spiritual reservoir of salvation for all His people.

Now what immediately follows from this?

You say, and quite correctly so: it follows that one must be connected, united with Christ in order to receive salvation. If your home is not properly wired and connected with the central electric plant in your city, you turn the switch in your living room quite in vain. You will have no light. If from the gas main pipes do not conduct the gas into your house, it is of no avail that you put a beautiful gas stove in your kitchen, or gas furnace in your basement. You will have no heat. In vain do you turn the faucet to draw water, if your home is not connected at all with that central reservoir in your town. The same is true in our relation to Christ. If our soul is not spiritually connected with Him, Who is our light, life, righteousness, wisdom, knowledge, sanctification, and redemption, we shall never have light, righteousness, and peace. It will remain dark and miserable in our soul. We must therefore be literally joined with Christ, united with Him. We must be *in* Him, even as He must be *in* us, in order that He may become *our* righteousness, holiness, and eternal life, and in order that we may draw out of Him all the blessings of grace.

This is what Scripture teaches us. This is taught by the figure of the vine and the branches. The branches must be in the vine in order to bear fruit. Christ is the vine; believers, and that, too, in their generations, are the branches. The branches are nothing except for their organic union with the vine. Even as it is the vine that bears fruit in and through the branches, so believers can bear fruit only because Christ lives and bears fruit in them. The same truth is taught us by the figure of the church as the body of Christ. Christ is the Head; the church is His body. And it is only from and by the Head that the body lives. Further, what is true of the body as a whole is equally true of the believers individually as members of that body. They have no life in themselves. Only in virtue of their organic union with the body do they live. For this reason the Bible speaks of believers as being *in* Christ. For of God they are in Christ Jesus, Who is made unto them wisdom, and righteousness, and sanctification, and redemption. (I Corinthians 1:30) And as in Adam all die, so in Christ all shall be made alive. (I Corinthians 15:22) And "if any man be in Christ, he is a new creature: old things are passed away; behold all things are become new." (II Corinthians 5:17) The saints are called "the faithful in Christ Jesus." (Ephesians 1:1) And they were sometimes darkness, but now they are light in the Lord. (Ephesians 5:8) And we are admonished to abide in Him, that we may bear much fruit. (John 15:4; I John 2:28)

This, then, is the first and absolutely indispensable requirement of

our salvation: we must be in Christ. Hence, we must be incorporated
into Him; we must be united with Him. A spiritual union must be
established between Christ and our soul, before we can receive any
fruit of Christ's death and resurrection. This union is absolutely first.
Unless that living connection is established between Christ and our inmost heart, we are outside of Him. And outside of Christ there is only
guilt and damnation, corruption and death, darkness and desolation.
Before there can be the faintest spark of new life in us, before there can
appear even the faintest glimmer of light in our soul, before the
simplest prayer can be uttered from our lips, before even the slightest
longing can arise in our soul for God and His Christ, that union must be
accomplished. It is an absolute prerequisite for the reception of all
salvation. For Christ is our all, and all our salvation is in Him. But we
cannot begin to draw our life and light, our knowledge and wisdom, our
righteousness and sanctification, from Him until our inmost heart is
joined in spiritual unity with Him, Who is the revelation of the God of
our salvation.

But how is this union accomplished?

The answer of Scripture is unequivocally: this union is unconditionally and absolutely the work of God's grace in Christ Jesus. By
grace are ye saved! That implies, too, that by grace, and by grace only,
you are incorporated into Christ, so that you become one plant with
Him.

When we say this, we proclaim nothing new. But we do wipe the
dust of oblivion from a very old, very fundamental, and very precious
truth. And we do claim that this truth is in dire need of a new emphasis over against many false representations, not by modernists, but by
those who claim that they preach the doctrine of salvation by grace.
For very many directly teach, or indirectly leave the impression by the
way they preach, that this first touch of the soul of the sinner with
Christ is accomplished by the sinner himself, or, at least, is contingent
for its establishment upon the will and choice of the sinner. Yes, they
admit, Christ is our salvation; and the soul must be united with Christ
in order to receive salvation. But if this union is to be accomplished,
the sinner must come to Christ. The Savior is willing to receive him, to
come into his heart, to join that sinner unto Himself; but the sinner
must first come. He must accept Christ. Or he must be willing to

receive Him. Or he must long and pray for this coming of Christ into his heart. And it seems that very sensational preaching, accompanied preferably by a heart-touching hymn and by begging and praying on the part of the preacher, is especially considered to be conducive to persuade the sinner to come to Jesus, to open the door of his heart, and to let Jesus come in. In last analysis, the union of the soul with the living Lord depends not on efficacious grace, but on the will of the sinner!

But, first of all, how absurd and utterly impossible is this presentation of salvation! If it were true, no man would be saved! For according to Scripture, the natural man is in the flesh; and the mind of the flesh is death. It is enmity against God; it is not subject to the law of God, neither indeed can be. Man is dead in sin and misery. He can neither perform nor will that which is good. He loves iniquity, and he is a slave of sin. He loves darkness rather than light. He cannot see the kingdom of God. Such is the natural man. Such is every man before that union with Christ is established of which we made mention. Do you expect that man to open his heart to Christ? Do you insist that this dead sinner must come to Christ before Christ will come to Him? Do you still maintain that this darkened sinner must at least long for Christ, hunger and thirst for Him, seek Him, ask for Him, before his soul can be united with the living Lord? I reply that if such were the truth, then could no man be saved. For before the sinner is united with Christ he can neither come to Him, nor long for Him, nor seek Him, nor utter the weakest prayer beseeching Him to come into his heart. But thanks be to God, this is not the truth! Salvation is not of man, nor of the will of man; nor does our union with Christ depend on man's consent. "No man can come unto me, except the Father which hath sent me draw him." (John 6:44) Again: "Therefore said I unto you, that no man can come unto me, except it were given unto him of my Father." (John 6:65)

And the Father does draw, and the Father does give, and the Father does unite us with the living Lord! And He does so, too, through Christ Himself, Who is exalted and draws all unto Him. He draws with cords of love, with irresistible power of grace. And when we are so drawn and so united with Christ, and He by His Spirit lives in us, we respond. We hunger and thirst, we long and pray, we come and embrace Him,

we eat the bread of life and are satisfied, we drink the water of life and
thirst nevermore, we draw from Him Who is the fulness of all the
blessings of salvation, even grace for grace!   All this is the fruit and
manifestation in us of that marvelous, mysterious, blessed wonder of
grace, of grace sovereign and free, whereby we are united with Christ.
For by grace are ye saved, through faith, and that not of yourselves:
it is the gift of God!

Blessed be the God and Father of our Lord Jesus Christ, Who has
blessed us with all spiritual blessings in heavenly places in Christ,
according as He hath chosen us in Him before the foundation of the
world!

Chapter 5

REGENERATED BY GRACE

> ... Verily, verily, I say unto
> thee, Except a man be born again,
> he cannot see the kingdom of God.
> — John 3:3

When the scion, or branch, of a fruit tree is grafted upon the trunk of another tree, the very first result of that organic union is that the nature and life of the tree begins to impart itself to the ingrafted scion. This first result is quite hid from our view. It is a mysterious operation. In fact, for a time the very opposite may present itself to the observing eye of the husbandman. It may appear as if the ingrafted shoot is dying because of the operation, and whatever buds or sprouts appeared on it before the ingrafting may wither. Yet the fact is, if the grafting is successful, that the ingrafted twig receives the beginning of a new life by virtue of its union with the trunk.

The same is true of the sinner who is united with Christ. He is a branch of the wild tree of the guilty and corrupt human race. He has a wild nature and brings forth wild and corrupt fruit. And Christ is that new, cultivated trunk, the root of a new tree. When that dead and wild sinner is united with, ingrafted into Christ, the very first result of that union is that the new nature and life of Christ is imparted to that corrupt sinner. He is principally renewed. Spiritually he has become another man. Also this principal change may not become at once apparent. He may not at once become conscious of the profound change that is wrought within him. Perhaps he does not come immediately to repentance and conscious faith. But the fact is there: if any man be in Christ, he is a new creation: old things are passed away, behold, all things have become new! (II Corinthians 5:17)

41

This first and profound change the Scriptures call the rebirth, or
the regeneration, of the sinner. Frequently and in different ways the
Bible refers to this rebirth. Of those who have received power to become the sons of God John writes: "Which were born, not of blood,
nor of the will of the flesh, nor of the will of man, but of God." (John
1:13) This implies nothing less than that the rebirth is that exclusively
divine work whereby God imparts His own nature to us, so that we become like Him, as His sons. To Nicodemus the Savior says: "Verily,
verily, I say unto thee, Except a man be born again, he cannot see the
kingdom of God." (John 3:3) This clearly teaches us that regeneration
is the absolutely indispensable condition for all spiritual activity. Before a man is regenerated, he can do nothing positive in regard to the
spiritual things of the kingdom of God. In I Peter 1:3 the apostle
writes that we have been begotten again unto a lively hope through the
resurrection of Jesus Christ from the dead, and that, too, according to
the abundant mercy of God. And in verse 23 of the same chapter we
read that we are "born again, not of corruptible seed, but of incorruptible, by the word of God, which liveth and abideth for ever." In his
first epistle the apostle John frequently emphasizes that believers are
born of God. "Whosoever is born of God doth not commit sin; for his
seed remaineth in him: and he cannot sin, because he is born of God."
(I John 3:9) And: "If ye know that he is righteous, ye know that
every one that doeth righteousness is born of him." (I John 2:29) And
once more: "We know that whosoever is born of God sinneth not."
(I John 5:18) Hence, believers are frequently called children of God,
not only in the juridical sense so that they are adopted to be sons of
God, but also in the spiritual sense, according to which they partake of
the divine nature and are conformed according to the image of His Son.
This change is so fundamental that one who is in Christ is called a new
creation. (II Corinthains 5:17) And it is nothing less than the resurrection from the dead: "Verily, verily, I say unto you, The hour is
coming, and now is, when the dead shall hear the voice of the Son of
God: and they that hear shall live." (John 5:25)

Now what is this marvelous work of grace that is called the rebirth
or regeneration of the sinner? Is it something like a moral reformation,
the building of character, the making of a better moral man? Is it the
same as conversion? Does regeneration in any sense depend upon man's

choice? Does the sinner in any way or to any degree cooperate in his own regeneration? These are important questions: for on our answer to them depends the true conception of salvation by grace only.

In general we may state, as is abundantly evident from all the passages of Scripture which we quoted, that regeneration is that wonderful work of God's grace whereby the sinner is raised from spiritual death to spiritual life in principle. Without entering into a detailed exposition let us note the following main points:

First of all, regeneration, or rebirth, reminds us forcibly that by virtue of his first birth man is dead. He is born dead. For why should the Scriptures otherwise emphasize that he must be born again? Or how otherwise could the Bible speak of this first change of the sinner as resurrection? Besides, that the sinner is dead in sin the Word of God abundantly testifies. Now what does it mean that the natural man is dead? It surely does not mean that he does not possess natural life or that through sin he changed into a different being. That he lives in a natural sense is evident: for he moves about in this world and accomplishes many mighty works. He thinks and wills, he plans and plots, he discovers and invents, he sees and hears and speaks and acts and reacts upon the world about him. But spiritually, that is in relation to God and all that is good, he is dead. His whole nature is corrupt. Sin is not a matter of the deed alone. If this were the case, he would need education and reformation. But spiritual death means that the very nature of the sinner is corrupt. His mind is darkened, so that he cannot discern the good. His will is perverse and obdurate, so that he cannot choose the good. All his inclinations are impure and defiled, so that he cannot have his delight in the good. But spiritual death means still more. The sinner is not a stock and block that is entirely passive, inactive. He is much worse. For, his heart, whence are the issues of life, being corrupt, his mind being darkened, and his will being perverse, he hates that which is good and loves the darkness rather than the light. With respect to the gospel and the things of the kingdom of God, this means that the natural man lacks the *power*, the *faculty*, to discern them. He has no eye to see, no ear to hear, no mind to discern, no will to long and to choose for them. He cannot accept Christ, and no amount of persuasion can induce him to accept Christ. He cannot hunger and thirst for righteousness. On the contrary, in that natural condition he will always react against the gospel, resist the Holy Spirit, and reject the Christ of God. Unless a man be born again, he *cannot see* the kingdom of God. But, secondly, we must make one more observation regarding the state of the natural man. He is not only dead in sin; he is also *earthy*. He was taken from the dust of the earth, and to the earth he is related and bound. This does not mean that Adam in his state of rectitude did not love God and seek His glory in all things. But it does imply that the heavenly things, those things which eye hath not seen, and ear hath not heard, and which have never arisen in the heart of man, were hid from him, too. Hence, even if the natural man were not dead in sin, he is still earthly and would still have to receive new powers in order to discern the heavenly things of God's kingdom and aspire after them. This, too, is presupposed in regeneration: for let us remember that the new birth is resurrection; and resurrection is not a return to a former life, but the raising to a higher, heavenly level of life.

In the third place, regeneration is that change in man which *empowers* him to see and to seek the kingdom of God. It is not the same as conversion, and it must not be confused with it. In conversion man is active: he begins to use the power and faculties which are given him in regeneration. He becomes conscious of the new life. He repents, confesses, turns about, hungers and thirsts after the bread and water of life, believes and embraces Christ and all His benefits, flees from sin and pursues after the good. But this is not the new birth itself, but it is the *activity* of the spiritually newborn babe. When a child is born, it is active: it cries and moves and kicks and seeks mother's breast and takes nourishment. But the faculties and powers to do all these things that child received in its conception and birth. The same is true of the reborn sinner. He is a newborn babe in a spiritual sense. He must be born again before he can act. He must have eyes before he can see, ears before he can hear, a spiritual faculty before he can discern, a new will before he can long for and accept the things of the kingdom of God. He must have the power of faith before he can believe, the gift of repentance before he can repent; and the love of God must be spread abroad in his heart before he can respond in love. This power is instilled into the heart of the sinner in the new birth, or regeneration. In regeneration God, by the efficacy of the Spirit, "opens the closed, and softens the hardened heart, and circumcises that which was uncircumcised, infuses new qualities into the will, which though heretofore dead, he quickens; from being evil, disobedient, and refractory, he renders it good, obedient, and pliable; actuates and strengthens it, that like a good tree, it may bring forth the fruits of good actions." (Canons of Dordrecht, III, IV, 11) By grace are ye saved, through faith, and that, (that is, that power of faith), not of yourselves, it is the gift of God.

Moreover, this new birth is a birth from above. It is resurrection. A new principle of life is instilled into our hearts by the wonder of regeneration. And this new life is not earthly, but heavenly; it is not from below, but from above. It is a beginning of the resurrection; it is a principle of the resurrection-life of Christ Himself! Hence, through regeneration we are empowered not only to seek after righteousness but to aspire after the heavenly things of the kingdom of God. In virtue of that new life, we become principally strangers and pilgrims in the earth, and seekers of the city that hath foundations, whose builder and artificer is God.

In the fourth place, in view of all that has been said about the new birth, it should be perfectly evident that it is a sovereign work of God pure and simple, a work in which the sinner himself has no part whatever, in which he does not in any sense cooperate with God, but in which man is wholly passive. It is important that this be emphasized in order to maintain the truth of salvation by grace only. All the more important this is, in view of the fact that in our day this truth is usually distorted and misrepresented. Those who insist on presenting salvation as contingent upon man's will do not know what to make of this new birth, though they often speak of it. Rebirth as a new creation, or as resurrection from the dead, has no place in their conception of salvation. Hence, they make of regeneration something which depends upon the will of the sinner. If man will only accept Christ, he will be regenerated. They offer to the sinner regeneration! They plead with him and beg him to be regenerated! But this is absurd. As well might a man go to the cemetery and beg the dead to come out of their graves! For no more than Adam cooperated in his own creation, and no more than Lazarus cooperated in his own resurrection, no more does the sinner cooperate with God in his own regeneration. It is a work of God alone, without our help. For "this is the regeneration so highly celebrated in Scripture, and denominated a new creation: a resurrection from the dead, a making alive, which God works in us without our aid. But this is in no wise effected merely by the external preaching of the gospel, by moral suasion, or such a mode of operation, that after God has performed his part, it still remains in the power of man to be regenerated or not, to be converted or to continue unconverted; but it is evidently a supernatural work, most powerful, and at the same time most delightful, astonishing, mysterious, and ineffable; not inferior in efficacy to creation, or the resurrection from the dead." (Canons of Dordrecht III, IV, 12)

In the fifth place, this truth is of great practical significance. For, first of all, this work being absolutely the work of God, in which the sinner is wholly passive, it is evident that there is no age limit to those who may become the recipients of this wonderful blessing of grace. The most hardened sinner, though he be hoary with age, may be regenerated; but also the infant at his mother's breast may receive this grace of God. In fact, there is good reason to believe that within the sphere of the church God usually regenerates the seed of the covenant in their early infancy. Not only, is there no reason to despair of their salvation if they die in infancy, even though they never heard the gospel; but this truth also requires of us as a church, and as parents, that we bring up our children in the sphere of the gospel and instruct them in the fear of the Lord from their earliest childhood. On mother's breast the child may learn to stammer his prayer; on mother's lap he must be instructed in the first knowledge of the gospel. And as he grows older, he must consistently be instructed in the Word of God, not only in the home, and in the church, but also in the school. Christian instruction is not only a calling: it is also a possibility, thanks be to God and His wonderful work of the new birth!

Secondly, this marvelous mystery of the new birth being wholly of divine authorship, we may rest assured that it can never be lost or undone. It might be destroyed as far as we are concerned: for how often we sin and make ourselves unworthy of the grace of God! But God never changes. Once regenerated is always regenerated. For let us remember that this work of grace is wrought by the God of our salvation *through Jesus Christ our Lord*. It is the first fruit of our being united with Him. It is only in union with Him that we receive this new principle of life. But even after we are reborn we do not possess the new life in ourselves. It is always in Christ, and out of Christ it constantly flows into our hearts by the indwelling Spirit. It remains dependent upon our union with the Savior. But this is exactly why it is safe and secure. For He will never leave us. And nothing can ever separate us from His love! The gifts of God are without repentance!

Chapter 6

CALLED BY GRACE

> Moreover whom he did pre-
> destinate, them he also called.
> — Romans 8:30

In the previous chapter we discussed regeneration, or the new birth. We explained that regeneration is that marvelous work of God through the Spirit of Christ whereby the sinner is translated from death into life. The new birth is a spiritual resurrection. It is the implanting of a principle of new life. That new life is different from the old life of sin not only in that it is holy but also in that it is heavenly. The new birth is a birth from above. Through it we become spiritual citizens of the New Jerusalem and, in principle, strangers in the earth.

But suppose now that no other operations of grace followed that of regeneration: would such a regenerated sinner of himself develop into a conscious and living believer in Christ? In the new birth the sinner receives new spiritual powers or faculties, the power of faith, and the power to repent, the power to embrace Christ and all His benefits. But if nothing else is done to that reborn sinner, will those powers of themselves spring into activity, so that the sinner now actually believes and repents, enters into the state of reconciliation, and receives the forgiveness of sins? Perhaps you reply: of course not, such a regenerated man must be brought into contact with the gospel! Well, suppose then, that you give him a Bible to read, or that some preacher instructs him and makes him acquainted with the truth as it is in Christ Jesus, will he merely through that contact with the Scriptures come to conscious saving faith, so that he actually repents and believes? Not at all. The wonderful work of regeneration as we discussed it in the previous chapter must be followed by another stage in the great work of salvation, a work, too, which is accomplished by the same Spirit Who regenerated the sinner. The seed of the new life that was implanted into his heart must be quickened into activity if it is to bear fruit, by the *calling*. The sinner must be called by grace.

Very often we read in the Bible of this calling of the sinner. The apostle Paul writes that "the gifts and calling of God are without repentance." (Romans 11:29) To the Corinthians he writes: "For ye see your calling, brethren, how that not many wise men after the flesh, not many mighty, not many noble, are called." (I Corinthians 1:26) And in Hebrews 3:1 the "holy brethren" are called "partakers of the heavenly calling." The apostle Peter admonishes us: "Wherefore the rather, brethren, give diligence to make your calling and election sure." (II Peter 1:10) The Lord Jesus tells us that He is "not come to call the righteous, but sinners to repentance." (Matthew 9:13) The saints are named "the called of Christ Jesus," and they are "called to be saints," and "the called according to his purpose." (Romans 1:6, 7; 8:28) In I Corinthians 1:23, 24 the apostle states that the preaching of Christ crucified is a stumbling block to the Jews, and foolishness to the Greeks, "But unto them which are called, both Jews and Greeks, Christ the power of God, and the wisdom of God." God's people are a chosen generation, a royal priesthood, an holy nation, a peculiar people, that they "should shew forth the praises of him who hath called (them) out of darkness into his marvelous light." (I Peter 2:9) And they are called unto glory and virtue. (II Peter 1:3) And not only do the Scriptures thus directly speak of the calling, but they also furnish us with concrete illustrations of what this calling should be. They call the sinner to repent and believe, the thirsty to drink, the hungry to eat, the weary to rest, the wicked to turn from his evil way.

"Ho, everyone that thirsteth, come ye to the waters, and he that hath no money, come ye, buy wine and milk without money and without price." (Isaiah 55:1) "Look unto me, and be ye saved, all the ends of the earth." (Isaiah 45:22) "Turn ye, turn ye from your evil ways; for why will ye die, O house of Israel?" (Ezekiel 33:11) "Come unto me, all ye that labor and are heavy laden, and I will give you rest." (Matthew 11:28) "Repent ye therefore, and be converted." (Acts 3:19) "Believe on the Lord Jesus Christ, and thou shalt be saved." (Acts 16:31)

You see from all this how important is the *calling* as a part of the work of salvation by grace. It is through this calling that the sinner comes to true repentance, so that he is filled with sorrow after God, that he comes to the water of life to drink, and to the bread of life to eat, that he is translated from darkness into light, from the state of enmity into that of reconciliation with God, and that he believes on the Lord Jesus Christ and is saved. Without and apart from this calling, the gospel of the crucified Christ is a stumblingblock to him, foolishness, and a savor of death unto death; but through the saving efficacy of this calling all this is changed, so that Christ becomes the power and the wisdom of God, and the gospel is a savor of life unto life unto the sinner.

The calling, then, is that work of God's mighty grace in Christ, through the Spirit, and by the preaching of the gospel, whereby the sinner is changed from darkness into light, so that he repents and consciously embraces Christ and all His benefits.

There are a few elements in this wonder of salvation to which we must call attention.

First of all, it may be emphasized that this calling always takes place *through the preaching of the Word.* For, "How then shall they call on him in whom they have not believed? and how shall they believe in him of whom they have not heard? and how shall they hear without a preacher? And how shall they preach, except they be sent?" (Romans 10:14, 15) About this important point I want to make a few remarks. A preacher is a man who is authorized by Christ to speak in His name, and through whom it pleases Christ to speak His own Word to men. Hence, he must be sent. The sinner must hear *Christ* speak to him. He must not hear the voice of a preacher, the voice of a mere man, but the voice of Jesus say to him: "Come unto me, and rest." The text which I just quoted is more correctly translated in the American Revised Version: "How shall they believe in him whom (not: of whom) they have not heard?" The dead must hear the voice of the Son of God. (John 5:25) The sheep must hear the voice of the Good Shepherd. (John 10:3, 27) The word of a mere man has no power, even though he should quote the Scriptures. Of what avail would it be if *I* would say to you that you must repent? Would you not say to me that I had better mind my own business? Or what would be the effect of *my* word, if *I* would assure you that Christ died for *you?*

Would that be a sound basis of faith for you? Or does it help any if *I* bid you come to Christ? But if Christ Himself speaks to you and causes His mighty Word to reach your inmost heart, you will repent, come to Him, believe, follow. "My sheep hear my voice, and I know them, and they follow me." (John 10:27)

Now it pleases Christ to cause His own voice to be heard through the preaching of the Word. And therefore, not everyone whom it pleases to assume the authority to preach is for that reason a preacher. A preacher must be sent. "How shall they preach except they be sent?" He must be called and commissioned by the Lord Christ Himself to preach. But how can anyone be sure that he is sent by Christ, that he may appear as Christ's ambassador, and that therefore Christ will speak His own mighty and living Word through his preaching? The answer of the Bible is very clear on this point: Christ sent and commissioned His apostles, and through them, His church to preach the gospel to all nations and every creature. This is very specific. The preaching of the gospel is not left to the whim and the choice of any individual who may take a fancy to preaching, but it is enjoined upon and entrusted to the church. To the church He gave His Spirit, that He might lead her into all the truth; and to that church He also entrusted His Word, that she might keep it, preserve it, and proclaim it even unto the ends of the earth. And the church accomplishes this holy calling through the ministry which the Lord Himself instituted. He, therefore, whom Christ calls through His church is a preacher, and no one else.

Such a preacher is, as far as his message is concerned, strictly bound to the Word of God as contained in the Holy Scriptures. He may not add, nor subtract, a tittle or iota from that Word; nor may he change it to suit the fancy of his audience. The full counsel of God he must proclaim, nothing less, and no more. Well may this truth be emphasized in our day. For, on the one hand, many a modern pulpit is changed into a rostrum for human philosophy; and many who are supposed to be ministers of the Word proclaim only the word of man, which is vain. Lectures on every conceivable subject are delivered from the place where the gospel is supposed to be preached. Men even designate special Sundays for that purpose, such as victory-Sundays, war bond-Sundays, Red Cross-Sundays, Community Chest-Sundays, Fathers' and Mothers' Day-Sundays, and what not. On the other hand, there are not a few in our day, not only men, but even women and children, who preach without being called, either on their own initiative and responsibility, or as sent out by some society or institute which operates apart from the church. These so-called preachers prefer to travel through the whole country, advertise themselves in the local papers, preferably announce the strangest topics in order to draw a crowd, and aim at stirring up a wave of emotionalism which they like to call a spiritual revival. They one and all hawk Christ as if He were the cheapest article on the religious market. This is a great evil: for thus the Word of God is corrupted.

Let the church beware! To her has been entrusted the calling to preserve and preach the pure Word of God through which Christ sends forth His own calling, and gathers His church.

But, in the second place, even though the calling takes place through the preaching of the gospel, it is not that preaching, nor the preacher, but Christ Who calls through the preaching and by His own Spirit. In fact, unless Christ Himself calls, there is no preaching. Christ, Who died and rose again, Who is exalted at the right hand of God, and Who received the promise of the Holy Ghost, is not only the contents of the gospel; He is also our Chief Prophet, Who calls His own unto salvation by His mighty Word. It is He Who gathers His church out of the whole world, not we. Even though it pleases Him to call men out of darkness into His light *through the preaching* by men, it is still He Who calls. He opens the eyes of the blind so that they see; He gives the hearing ear to hear the voice of the Good Shepherd; He enlightens the mind so that we may understand the things of the kingdom of God; He inclines the will and the heart to give heed to the Word of truth. The calling is a work of God through Christ. By grace are ye saved also means that by grace ye are called.

This, too, may well be emphasized in our day. On the one hand, he who preaches the gospel must constantly bear this in mind, in order that he may be humble. He must not leave the impression by the way he preaches as if he were the whole show, as if he were really the one who calls and saves souls, while the Holy Spirit is a sort of assistant evangelist who is called in at the right moment to finish the preacher's work. He is only an instrument. But on the other hand, the audience, too, must understand that the important point of the sermon is not that it pleases them, that it is a "nice sermon," by which they were probably entertained for forty-five minutes. But the great question is whether through the preaching they heard the calling of Christ the Lord, the voice of Jesus saying, "Come unto me, and rest." The calling is through the preaching, but it is of God through Christ. By grace are ye called!

Thirdly, and in close connection with what was just said, it must be strongly emphasized that this calling unto salvation is indeed a *divine calling,* and that, therefore, it comes to us with *authority* and *power.* It is not a weak human plea, nor a mere invitation which one may either accept or reject, nor a generous offer which one may receive or decline: it is the Word of God that comes to the sinner when Christ calls through the preaching. And "the word of God is quick, and powerful, and sharper than any two-edged sword, piercing even to the dividing asunder of soul and spirit, and of the joints and marrow, and is a discerner of the thoughts and intents of the heart." (Hebrews 4:12) And again: "So shall my word be that goeth forth out of my mouth: it shall not return unto me void, but it shall accomplish that which I please, and it shall prosper in the thing whereto I sent it." (Isaiah 55:11) The preacher must be conscious of the fact that he is a minister of the mighty Word of God; and he may not leave the impression that Christ is a poor and weak beggar, Who would fain persuade men to open their hearts to Him and let Him in, but Who is powerless to enter if they refuse. In much of our modern preaching there is no longer the note of authority and power; and men, instead of being convicted of sin, and humbled in dust and ashes, receive the impression that they really would do Christ quite a favor if they would leave their wicked way and repent. God's calling is authoritative. When He says to you, "Repent!" woe, if you do not! But God's calling is also powerful. When through the preaching of the Word, He enters into your inmost soul and calls you, it is no longer in your power not to repent and not to return from your wicked way. For the Word of God is quick and powerful; it accomplishes all God's good pleasure.

Finally, this divine calling is always effectual. This does not mean that the preacher may expect that all who come under the external preaching of the Word are also called unto salvation. Always there is a twofold effect; the preaching is a savor of death unto death, as well as a savor of life unto life. But the elect are surely called. They receive the hearing ear, the seeing eye, the willing heart. They hear the Word of God, and they tremble. They are sorry for their sins, and repent. They cry out, "God be merciful to me, a sinner," and receive forgiveness. They hear the voice of Jesus say to them personally, "Come unto me, and I will give you rest!" And they come to Him and do find rest. They hear the voice of the Good Shepherd and know that they are of His sheep. And they follow Him, and He gives them eternal life; and they shall never perish, neither shall any man pluck them out of His hand. For the gifts of God and the calling are without repentance. For "whom he did predestinate, them he also called: and whom he called, them he also justified: and whom he justified, them he also glorified." (Romans 8:30)

We are called by irresistible grace unto virtue and eternal glory!

Chapter 7

BELIEVING THROUGH GRACE

> ... and that not of yourselves:
> it is the gift of God.
>
> — Ephesians 2:8

We are saved by grace and through faith. Another way than that of faith in Jesus Christ, the Christ of the Scriptures, Who was delivered for our transgressions and raised for our justification, there is not.

This is the clear testimony of Scripture throughout.

For "as Moses lifted up the serpent in the wilderness, even so must the Son of Man be lifted up: That whosoever believeth in him should not perish, but have eternal life. For God so loved the world, that he gave his only begotten Son, that whosoever believeth in him should not perish, but have everlasting life." (John 3:14-16) "He that believeth on him is not condemned: but he that believeth not is condemned already, because he hath not believed in the name of the only begotten Son of God." (John 3:18) And again: "He that believeth on the Son has everlasting life: and he that believeth not the Son shall not see life; but the wrath of God abideth on him." (John 3:36) When the Jews inquire of the Savior what work they must do in order to obtain the bread that never perishes, the Lord answers: "This is the work of God, that ye believe on him whom he hath sent." (John 6:29) And to Martha, the sister of Lazarus, the Lord addresses the marvelous words: "I am the resurrection, and the life: he that believeth in me, though he were dead, yet shall he live: And whosoever liveth and believeth in me shall never die. Believest thou this?" (John 11:25, 26) Hence, when the kingdom of God is at hand, the summons goes forth: "Repent ye, and believe the gospel." (Mark 1:15) And the apostles go out into all the world with the message, "Believe in the Lord Jesus Christ, and thou

57

shalt be saved." (Acts 16:31)   Paul is "not ashamed of the gospel of Christ: for it is the power of God unto salvation to every one that believeth." (Romans 1:16)   And "if thou shalt confess with thy mouth the Lord Jesus, and shalt believe in thine heart that God hath raised him from the dead, thou shalt be saved." (Romans 10:9) The sole way of salvation, according to the Scriptures, is faith in the Lord Jesus Christ, crucified and raised from the dead.

It is an important question, therefore: what is this faith in the Lord Jesus Christ, and what does it mean to believe in Him?

Is it a natural power, something which every man possesses and which he may either use or refuse to employ?   There is, indeed, a certain natural faith, which is not unto salvation.   It is a mere, intellectual assent to the truth.   Every man, even the most pronounced and profane atheist, believes in his deepest heart that God is: the devils believe, too, and they tremble.   And so one may believe the facts of the gospel, without ever being concerned about them.   I may believe that the Son of God came into the flesh without knowing Him as the light of the world and of my soul.   I may assent to the truth of His crucifixion without fleeing to that cross for my personal redemption and washing my garments in His blood.   And thus, one may believe that the facts of revelation are true without having any spiritual part in them.   Such faith is no power.   It is a faith of the head, not of the heart.   Or rather, it is a faith of the natural man, not of the regenerated child of God.   It is barren, it bears no fruit.   Such natural faith does not reveal itself in true sorrow after God and repentance, and it is not the power of a new life.

But true faith, through which we are saved, is different.

It is, let us notice first of all, faith in Jesus Christ.   That means that it is faith in God through Christ, or faith in God as He revealed Himself in our Lord Jesus Christ as the God of our salvation.   Christ is the revelation of God.   In Him God makes Himself known to us as JEHOVAH-SALVATION.   The center of this revelation, the focal point of this glorious light of salvation that shines from the face of God, is the resurrection of Jesus Christ from the dead.   Notice that the apostle writes in Romans 10:9 that he who "believeth in his heart that God raised him from the dead, shall be saved."   In creation God reveals Himself as the Lord Omnipotent, Who calls the things that are not as if they were; in the resurrection of Jesus Christ from the dead, He makes Himself known as Jehovah-Salvation, Who quickeneth the dead. Hence, in the fifteenth chapter of I Corinthians, the apostle emphasizes that if Christ were not raised, our faith would be vain, and we would still be in our sins. The resurrection of Jesus Christ from the dead is the precious cornerstone of our salvation.

Of course, this resurrection must not be conceived as an isolated fact, but as an inseparable element of the whole revelation of God in Christ. He who believes that God raised Jesus from the dead also believes that Christ is the only begotten Son of God, sent by the Father into the world, God with us, Immanuel. To believe that He was raised from the dead by the Father implies the faith that God laid our iniquities upon Him, and that He bore them as the Lamb of God that taketh away the sins of the world, so that "God was in Christ reconciling the world unto Himself, not imputing their trespasses unto them." It implies that the death of Christ on the accursed tree was vicarious, substitutional, that He died instead of and in behalf of all whom the Father had given Him; and that this death was atoning, fully satisfying for all our sins, so that the guilt of our sins is blotted out, and we are clothed with an eternal righteousness before God in Christ. For never would God have raised Him from the dead, Who bore all our iniquities, if He had not fully satisfied for them. And this Christ, Who was delivered for our transgressions, and raised for our justification, is exalted in the highest heavens, and sitteth at the right hand of God, clothed with power and majesty. To Him was given the promise of the Holy Spirit, that by His power all for whom He died might be drawn unto Him and obtain righteousness and life forever. This Jesus Christ, the Son of God in the flesh, crucified and raised, exalted at the right hand of God as the Lord of glory, is the revelation of the God of our salvation. And faith that saves is faith in God through Him. He that believeth that *God raised Jesus from the dead* shall be saved!

Secondly, we must observe that this saving faith is faith *in* or *into* Jesus Christ as the revelation of the God of our salvation. This is often emphasized in Scripture. We do read sometimes of believing *on* Jesus, and then the idea of faith as confidence appears to have the emphasis. But the true character of saving faith is expressed in the phrase: faith *in* Christ. He who has the true faith believes *into* Christ.

What does this signify?

It means that faith is that altogether mysterious and wonderful spiritual power whereby the soul strikes its roots into Christ, to cling to Him, appropriate Him, and draw out of Him all the glorious blessings of salvation which are in Him — the forgiveness of sins, eternal righteousness, and life. The difference between a believer and an unbeliever is not unlike that between a living young tree and a dead fence post. You can plant that fence post deep into the ground, but you do not expect that it will show signs of life and develop branches and fruit. On the contrary, it will rot in the soil in which it is planted. But plant a young sapling in the same soil, and it will strike its roots into the ground, draw nourishment from it, grow and bear fruit. The same is true of a living, saving faith in relation to Christ. Bring the unbelieving, dead sinner into contact with Christ as He is revealed in the Holy Scriptures, and there will be no saving reaction. On the contrary, there is a reaction of unbelief unto damnation. But if the believer is led to Christ through the preaching of the Word, he will take hold of Him, cling to Him, strike the roots of his entire soul into Him, and draw out of Him all the spiritual nourishment necessary unto eternal life. What the roots are for the young tree, saving faith is for the believer in Christ: by faith the believer is rooted in Him. And since Christ is revealed to us in the Scriptures, true faith always turns to them, has its delight in the Word of God, is called into activity through the Word preached, and constantly grows according as it increases in the knowledge and understanding of all that God has revealed to us in His Word.

The activity of a true and conscious faith, therefore, engages the entire soul, with mind and will and all our desires and inclinations. Through faith the whole soul fastens itself upon Christ.

Hence, faith is first of all a true spiritual knowledge of Christ as the revelation of the God of our salvation. This knowledge of faith must not be confused with a mere natural knowledge about Christ such as anyone may acquire by studying the Bible or by applying himself to dogmatics. This knowledge *about* Christ is indispensable, but itself is not the knowledge of a saving faith. The latter is spiritual, experiential. A scientist, whose stomach is full of cancer, may be able to tell you all about the ingredients and their food value of a gorgeous dinner you prepared before him; but the food is nauseating to him, and he cannot partake of it. The uneducated laborer, returning from his day's work, may know nothing about calories and vitamins; but he sits down at the table and takes delight in the food you prepare. So the unbeliever may know all about Christ. He may even be a scientific theologian, able to instruct others in the knowledge of salvation. But his knowledge is purely intellectual, natural, theoretical. He does not know Christ spiritually. He does not have his delight in Him, partake of Him, eat and drink Him. But the true believer, even though he may be far less equipped with theological knowledge, knows Christ spiritually. He does not merely know that he himself is a sinner; but he has a spiritual knowledge of his sin, is filled with true sorrow after God, repents and cries out, "God be merciful to me a sinner!" He knows the Lord Jesus Christ, not merely in the sense that he knows all about Him, but as the fulness of his own emptiness, as the righteousness of his own unrighteousness, as the light of his own darkness, as the life of his own death, as the bread of life for which he hungers, as the water of life for which he thirsts, as the way, the truth, and the life, by which he longs to come to the Father. He recognizes Him as his own Savior and Redeemer, longs for Him, eats and drinks Him unto righteousness and life. The believer knows Christ with the knowledge of love and delight!

And so, true faith is also a sure and hearty confidence, a believing *on* Christ, a relying on Him in life and in death, for time and for eternity. If I confide, trust in someone completely, I surrender myself entirely and unconditionally to him, assured of his love and good will toward me, and of his ability and wisdom to seek my good. If I must travel through a strange, mountainous country, where I do not know the way, and the danger of hidden ravines lurks on every side, and I employ a guide, I surrender myself entirely to him, trusting in his good will and ability to lead me through safely. But if I suspect his good intentions toward me, or doubt his knowledge of the right way, I will not confide in him and follow where he leads. Thus, saving faith is a hearty confidence. Its basis is the assurance that God is filled with an eternal and unchangeable love to me, a sinner, and that He is able to save to the uttermost. I am assured of this because He revealed His love in the cross of Jesus Christ, my Lord, as a love that is willing to go into the deepest woe of death and hell for me, while I was still an enemy of God. And He gloriously manifested His power to save in the resurrection of Christ from the dead. In that God of my salvation I trust. On God through Christ I rely, in life and in death, now and in the day of judgment, fully assured that all my sins are forgiven me, and that He gives me eternal righteousness and life for Christ His Son's sake. This spiritual knowledge of love and delight, this wholehearted and unconditional surrender to and reliance upon, the God of our salvation in Christ is the activity of saving faith.

From all that we have said about the nature and activity of saving faith it also should have become evident what is the relation between faith and salvation. He that believeth shall be saved, have everlasting life. But why? What is the relation between salvation and faith?

The impression is often left by preachers who present the matter of faith as something that depends on the sinner's own will and choice, as if faith were a *condition* unto salvation. God is willing to save us *on condition* that we believe. But there are no conditions to salvation. We are not saved on condition of faith, or on the ground of, or because of our faith. The only ground of our salvation is Jesus, crucified and raised. Nor are we saved through faith because faith is regarded as a good work, or because through faith we are able to do good works and obtain righteousness before God. For we are saved by grace; and if it is of works, it is no more of grace. It cannot even be said that faith is the hand whereby we take hold of the salvation that is offered us. Salvation is not an offer, but a wonder work of God; and the sinner has no hand to accept it. But faith is the means, and that, too, *God's* means, whereby we are implanted into Christ. It is the spiritual power whereby we cling to the God of our salvation in Jesus Christ our Lord, our righteousness and perfect redemption forever! By grace are ye saved, not on condition of, nor because of, but *through* faith, and that not of yourselves, it is the gift of God.

Yes, faith is by grace. It is the gift of God! This, too, should be perfectly evident from all that has been said about its nature and activity; but it is not superfluous to accentuate this truth. How often this truth is distorted in our day! How many there are who, even though they do not literally preach that faith is the work of man, leave the impression by their way of preaching, their pleading and begging, that it is in the power of any sinner to believe in Christ whenever he pleases, and to reject Him as he pleases! O, the matter is so simple and easy, say they. Just say that you accept Jesus as your personal Savior, and the thing is settled! And so they change the wonderwork of God into an arbitrary whim of the sinner's will. But it is not so. It is not of him that willeth, nor of him that runneth, but of God that showeth mercy. (Romans 9:16) Only when the Holy Spirit accomplishes the wonderwork of faith in the heart can the sinner accept Christ. And he in whom the Spirit has wrought the marvelous work of faith neither can nor will ever reject Him. And through that faith he is surely saved. Saved he is now: for he that believeth on the Son hath everlasting life. And saved he shall be in the day of the revelation of Jesus Christ: for he shall then be made like Him in resurrection glory.

By grace are ye saved, through faith, and that not of yourselves, it is the gift of God!

Chapter 8

JUSTIFIED BY GRACE

> ... and whom he called, them
> he also justified.
>
> — Romans 8:30

One of the greatest, and certainly the most fundamental, of all the blessings of salvation that are bestowed upon us through our Lord Jesus Christ by grace is that of justification.

In general, we may say that justification is the act of God whereby we become righteous before Him. It means that we stand before the judgment seat of God, as we always do; that God judges us, as He always does; that He applies the perfect standard of His holy will to us, to our being and nature, to our life and walk; that He expresses His verdict upon us, and that this verdict declares us free from all sin and guilt and perfectly righteous, so righteous as if we had never had any sin, as if we had always perfectly kept His every commandment. It also means that He inscribes that verdict by which He declares us righteous in our very hearts, so that we are conscious of it, are assured of our righteousness before God. This gift of grace is so fundamental and all important because it is the key to all other blessings of grace. For God loves the righteous, and He hates all the workers of iniquity. He cannot look with favor upon the ungodly. If, then, we are to become the objects of His loving kindness, it is prerequisite that we are righteous. And the possession and consciousness of this righteousness fills us with unspeakable joy and with a great and profound peace. "Even as David also describeth the blessedness of the man, unto whom God imputeth righteousness without works, Saying, Blessed are they whose iniquities are forgiven, and whose sins are covered. Blessed is the man unto whom the Lord will not impute sin." (Romans 4:6-8) And again:

65

"Therefore being justified by faith, we have peace with God through our Lord Jesus Christ." (Romans 5:1)

The wonder of this justification is that at the very moment when God declares us righteous, we are very really sinners, worthy of damnation in ourselves, and that of this we are deeply conscious. The believer who receives this grace of justification is a justified sinner. For "to him that worketh not, but believeth on him that justifieth the ungodly, his faith is counted for righteousness." (Romans 4:5) That is the great marvel of it.

It is very important that we clearly understand this. The justified sinner is not one who formerly was ungodly and therefore was the object of God's condemnation, but who has reformed, converted himself, become godly, pious, religious, and who now appears in the judgment of God with his new piety and good works, and on the basis of them is declared righteous. Not at all! The contrary is true. The justified sinner is very really a sinner in himself, and as such he appears in the moment of justification before the tribunal of God. He is an enemy of God. His nature is corrupt, and there is no good in him at all. He is wholly inclined to all evil. He has transgressed all the commandments of God and kept none of them. Yea, what is worse, at the very moment when he stands before the judgment seat of God, he sins and violates God's precepts. And he knows this. He carries the testimony in his own conscience that he is a sinner, worthy of damnation; that he is inclined to all evil and incapable of doing any good; that he trampled God's holy law under foot, and that even now, as he stands before God's holy judgment seat, he continues to transgress. He is deeply conscious of the fact that if God will enter into judgment with him and deal with him according to his nature and deserts, he cannot stand for a moment, but must expect that he will be sentenced to eternal damnation. All he can do, and even that he cannot and will not do of himself, is to cry out, "God be merciful to me, a sinner!" And the marvel of justification is that this sinner, who has nothing to bring before God but corruption and rebellion, is declared righteous before God, and hears the verdict that he has no sin, that all his sins are blotted out and forgiven, that he is clothed with a righteousness that makes him worthy of eternal life and glory. He is justified by grace!

Such is the clear teaching of Scripture. "For all have sinned, and come short of the glory of God; Being justified freely by his grace through the redemption that is in Christ Jesus." (Romans 3:23, 24) The sinner receives a righteousness that is not his own, but wholly of God, and that is given him, imputed to him, reckoned to him by grace. For, "by the deeds of the law there shall no flesh be justified in his sight: for by the law is the knowledge of sin. But now the righteousness of God without the law is manifested, being witnessed by the law and the prophets; Even the righteousness of God which is by faith of Jesus Christ unto all and upon all them that believe: for there is no difference." (Romans 3:20-22) All boasting is excluded, for "a man is justified by faith without the deeds of the law." (Romans 3:28) And even "as by the offence of one judgment came upon all men to condemnation; even so by the righteousness of one the free gift came upon all men unto justification of life. For as by one man's disobedience many were made sinners, so by the obedience of one shall many be made righteous." (Romans 5:18, 19) From all this it is abundantly evident that God is revealed as the God Who justifies the ungodly, and that the sinner is made righteous by a righteousness which is of God, without any works of righteousness on his part whatever.

But here several questions arise. The first of these is: how is it possible that God can justify the unjust? How can He pronounce a sentence of justification upon him who is guilty and corrupt? Does not Scripture teach everywhere that God is righteous and just, and that He will by no means clear the guilty? How then is it possible to believe in God as the God Who justifies the ungodly?

The answer of the Word of God is: through Jesus Christ our Lord. We are justified freely by His grace *through the redemption that is in Christ Jesus.* The righteousness that is ours through the grace of justification is *by faith of Jesus Christ.* It is in Christ that God revealed Himself as the God Who justifies the ungodly. Christ is the righteous one. In Him there is a righteousness that is so great and mighty that it blots out all our sins and clothes us with an eternal righteousness, makes us worthy of eternal life. In the judgment of God Christ took our place. He assumed full responsibility for us. All our sins He took upon Himself, and He bore them away for ever. For He not merely suffered the punishment for the sins of His own; but in suffering the wrath of God He was perfectly obedient, even unto the death of the cross. His death was an act. He laid down His life. He sacrificed Himself. Voluntarily, motivated by the love of God, He went down into lowest hell, that there He might bear the wrath of God against sin. And thus He satisfied the justice of God. He made an atonement. He removed the guilt of sin and merited eternal righteousness. And God justified Him and pronounced the verdict of perfect righteousness upon Him, when He raised Him from the dead and gave Him everlasting glory and immortality. In the death and resurrection of Jesus Christ from the dead God revealed Himself as the God Who justifies the ungodly. And if we believe on Him, we receive by that faith the sentence of God's justification in our hearts. For this righteousness of Christ is imputed to all those for whom Christ died and was raised, so that we are as perfectly righteous before God as if we ourselves had performed that act of obedience on the cross which Christ performed for us. And by faith we lay hold upon this verdict of justification, so that we know that even though all things testify against us in this world of sin and death, we are righteous before God and heirs of eternal life.

But another question arises here. How can the righteousness of Christ be reckoned as ours? Or how could, in the justice of God, Christ die for our sins? Do we not rather meet here with a double injustice, namely, that the righteous is punished, and the guilty is acquitted? If in a worldly court one is found guilty of murder, would a judge inflict capital punishment upon another instead of the guilty one, even though that other would voluntarily offer himself to take the murderer's place? Would that not be considered a double perversion of justice? Moreover, how can the death and obedience of the one be the righteousness of countless sinners?

But here we must remember that Christ is not merely another man, but He is the Son of God come into the flesh. No mere man has a life to substitute for another's: for his life is not his own, and, besides, he is himself a sinner under sentence of death. But Christ is the Son of God, very God Himself, Who took our flesh and blood upon Himself voluntarily. He became man by an act of His own will. He had power to lay down His life for others, if He so pleased. And before the world was, He had been appointed the Head of all the elect, so that He represented them and was responsible for them. By God's eternal decree of election they are one body, one legal corporation, represented by Christ

Who is their Head. Christ, therefore, can be summoned before the bar of God's judgment and appear there for all His own, assume responsibility for them, take all their guilt upon Himself, and pay for their sins by an act of perfect obedience on His part. And again, because He is not a mere man, but the Son of God in the flesh, His death is of immeasurable value, infinitely precious, capable of blotting out the sins of all His own and of procuring for them eternal righteousness and everlasting life and glory. This, then, is the marvelous grace of God in justifying the ungodly. He Himself came down to us, assumed our human nature, and in that human nature assumed responsibility for our sins, became obedient unto death, yea unto the death of the cross, thus blotting out the handwriting of our sins that was against us. In Christ He is the God Who justifies the ungodly. By grace are ye saved!

You say, perhaps, that we must believe in order to be justified before God, and that, therefore, it is faith that makes us righteous before God. And it is true enough that we are justified by faith only. He that believeth on Him Who justifies the ungodly is righteous, and he only. And that means that we must believe on God as He revealed Himself in Jesus Christ, crucified and raised from the dead. For this righteousness is imputed to us "if we believe on him that raised up Jesus our Lord from the dead." (Romans 4:24) There is no other way than that of faith to become righteous before God. We must try no other way. All our good works are but filthy works. All our own goodness and piety, our very religiousness and the very best of our religious acts must be utterly discarded as a ground of righteousness; and we must come before God as naked sinners, but believing on God Who justifieth the ungodly, if we would obtain righteousness and life. By faith we are justified. But let us beware, lest we make of faith another good work on our part on the ground of which we are justified. Faith is not the ground of our justification. We are not justified because we believe. Nor are we justified by faith because through faith we become holy and capable of doing good works. Christ crucified and raised is the only ground of our righteousness. And faith is only the means whereby we are united with Christ and the spiritual power whereby we lay hold on this righteousness, so that we know and wholly rely on God Who justifieth the ungodly.

Besides, let us not forget that faith itself is a gift of God. No man can or will of himself accept Christ and believe on God Who raised Him from the dead. God through Christ by His Spirit works within our hearts the justifying faith. And so it is all of grace. By grace God came down to us in our sin and death, and in the Person of His only begotten Son assumed our flesh and blood. By grace Christ died for our sins on the accursed tree and was raised on the third day for our justification. By grace God chose us and ordained us to eternal righteousness and life in Christ before the foundation of the world. And by grace He gives to us the power of faith, thus uniting us with Christ and causing us to believe on Him Who justifieth the ungodly. By grace are ye saved, through faith, and that not of yourselves: it is the gift of God!

But the objection might be and often is raised against this doctrine of free justification that it is dangerous and demoralizing. If it is true that whatever we do has no bearing on our righteousness before God, so that our sins do not prevent our justification and so that our good works cannot increase our righteousness, does it not follow that a justified sinner may well live and continue in sin?

Superficially considered, this conclusion would appear quite logical and inevitable. Just imagine: our works have nothing to do with the verdict of justification which God pronounces upon us! God justifies the ungodly! Though your sins be as scarlet, God's sentence is that you are righteous. Though you live the most painstaking life of godliness, you cannot add to this righteousness that is freely given you: for it is perfect in Christ. Well, then, will not a justified sinner conclude that he may as well live in sin, seeing that nothing can change his imputed righteousness? Nay, what is more, does not the doctrine that one is justified by mere grace directly lead to the conclusion that we ought to live in sin, in order that grace may abound? The enemies of this truth often raise this objection. They did so already in the days of the apostle Paul. Even then there were those who slanderously reported the apostles as teaching, "Let us do evil, that good may come." (Romans 3:8)

Yet this objection is without ground. For let us remember that we are justified out of faith and that by faith we are united with Christ and live out of Him. And it is quite impossible that one who lives out of Christ should deliberately continue in sin. He has died with Christ and is raised with Him unto newness of life. Hence, he condemns his own sin and hates it. He is dead to sin. By faith he repents and cries out, "God, be merciful to me, a sinner!" By faith he hungers and thirsts after righteousness and lays hold on the righteousness of Christ. And by that same faith he abhors the ways of sin and earnestly strives to walk in holiness in the midst of the present world, longing for the day when he shall be perfectly delivered from the body of this death, to sing the praises of His Redeemer, Who delivered him from the dominion of sin and called him out of darkness into His marvelous light!

Chapter 9

CONVERTED BY GRACE

... turn thou me, and I shall
be turned.
— Jeremiah 31:18

When we speak of the conversion of the sinner by grace, it may be well to consider for a moment the question as to the relation which this particular blessing of salvation sustains to the rest of God's wonderwork of grace whereby He redeems and delivers us from sin and death and makes us partakers of His eternal glory.

In the chapter on justification we remarked that this is the most fundamental blessing of grace: for God loves the righteous only; and therefore, unless we are justified, declared righteous by Him, we cannot expect any token of His favor. In this sense, that is, as the ground of all other blessings of salvation, justification is first. But this must not be misunderstood. It does not mean that in order of time the sinner first *receives* the gift of righteousness by faith, and that thereupon he is regenerated, united with Christ, called and converted. From God's viewpoint this is certainly true. Before God His people are justified from eternity; and He beholds them forever as perfectly righteous in Christ, and as such He blesses them. Moreover, this sentence of justification, our righteousness in Christ before God, was realized in the cross and resurrection of our Lord. And it is also true before the consciousness of the believer that by faith he first of all takes hold of this righteousness of Christ, the forgiveness of sins, before he dare hope for any other gift of God's grace. Yet the fact is, of course, that when the sinner performs that act of faith whereby he lays hold upon the righteousness of Christ, he is already reborn unto new life, called out of darkness into God's marvelous light, united with Christ in the Spirit;

and he has already received the gifts of faith and conversion. For it is only as a reborn, called, and believing sinner that he can embrace Christ as his righteousness. Even though justification is the ground of conversion, the justified sinner *is* a converted sinner.

The Scriptures frequently speak of this conversion of man, and they employ different terms to denote this wonder of grace. The Old Testament uses a word in the Hebrew which simply means "to turn" and is sometimes translated thus, while at other times it is rendered by our English "convert." "The law of the Lord is perfect, converting the soul." (Psalm 19:7) The psalmist vows that he will teach transgressors the way of Jehovah, and then sinners will be converted unto Him. (Psalm 51:13) "If the wicked will turn from all his sins" and keep God's law, he shall surely live. (Ezekiel 18:21) The house of Israel is called to turn themselves from idols and from all their abominations. (Ezekiel 14:6) The Lord has no pleasure in the death of the wicked, but in this, that he turn from his wicked way and live. Hence, the Word of the Lord comes to apostatizing Israel: "Turn ye, turn ye from your evil ways." (Ezekiel 33:11) They are exhorted to turn to their God and to keep mercy and judgment (Hosea 12:6); to turn unto Him with all their heart, for He is gracious and merciful, slow to anger and of great kindness. (Joel 2:12, 13)

In the New Testament two words are used for conversion. The one means approximately the same as our English word "conversion" or "convert" and denotes a complete turning about. The other really signifies a change of mind, that is, of the whole inner man, and is translated "repentance." The Lord says to His disciples: "Except ye be converted, and become as little children, ye shall not enter into the kingdom of heaven." (Matthew 18:3) John preached the baptism of repentance, that is, of an inner change in the sinner. (Mark 1:4; Luke 3:3) The apostles come to the people with the exhortation: "Repent ye therefore, and be converted." (Acts 3:19) And they preached that God had exalted Christ to be a Prince and Savior, "for to give repentance to Israel, and forgiveness of sins." (Acts 5:31) And the church in Jerusalem glorifies God, acknowledging that He "also to the Gentiles granted repentance and life." (Acts 11:18) And Paul was sent to the Gentiles "to open their eyes, and to turn them from darkness to light, and from the power of Satan unto God," and that "they should repent and turn to God, and do works meet for repentance." (Acts 26:18, 20) Moreover, conversion in the broader sense is called sanctification, cleansing, purification, the putting off of the old man and the putting on of the new man, the mortification of the deeds of the body, etc. (II Corinthians 7:1; I John 3:4; Ephesians 4:22-24; Romans 8:13)

From all these different passages of Holy Writ, and from many others, we may gather what is the Scriptural teaching concerning true conversion. First of all, we learn that it is a complete and radical turning about in a spiritual, ethical sense of the word. It is a turning from Satan to God, from enmity against God to the love of God in Christ, from darkness to light, from sin to righteousness, from corruption to holiness. By nature the sinner is motivated by enmity against God; and as a result, his whole life is directed in the way of darkness and sin. He loves the darkness rather than the light. His heart and mind and will, and all his desires and inclinations turn away from God and are enslaved to the will of the devil. Hence, also his outward life and walk is turned in the direction of unrighteousness. He walks away from God and contrary to His precepts. But in conversion he turns away from all this in order to turn to the living God. His hatred of God is changed into love, his darkness is turned into light, his love of iniquity is turned into a love of God's precepts, and his members which he yielded as instruments of unrighteousness he now yields as instruments of righteousness unto God. I stated that this conversion, this spiritual turning about, is complete. By this I mean that it is a turning about of the whole man, with his internal life as well as with his external walk. It is not an external reformation by virtue of which a man for some reason changes his external deportment, so that he who once was a drunkard now lives soberly, or one who lived in sexual abandonment now walks in chastity. But it is a turning about in our outward walk which is rooted in an inner change of the heart and mind, of the will, and of all the affections. And from this it also follows that conversion is a *radical* change. It is a break with sin as sin, and a turning to God for God's sake, a love of righteousness for righteousness' sake. It is, therefore, not a turning away from *some* sins and a keeping of *some* of God's precepts. It is hatred of *all* sins, and a fundamental delight in *all* the precepts of the Lord our God. This complete and radical turning about of the sinner is conversion.

From this it will also be evident that conversion has two aspects. The first of these is that it is a turning away from sin with all our heart and a fighting against sin. This, in general, is what the Bible means by the putting off of the old man, or the mortification of our members which are upon earth. Its chief characteristic is repentance, or true sorrow over sin. By this you may surely know that you are converted. If you wonder sometimes whether or not you are converted, it is well to ask yourself the question whether you are truly sorry for sin. For the chief characteristic of true conversion in this life is not that you are always on the mountain tops and perform many wonderful good works but that you repent in true sorrow after God. I say: *true* sorrow. For there is also a false, a counterfeit sorrow of the world. The two, however, may easily be distinguished from each other. For true sorrow is rooted in the love of God, while the sorrow of the world is really love of self. The former is sorrow over sin as sin, that is, because it is contrary to the will of God; the latter is sorrow over sin because of its evil consequences. Counterfeit sorrow over sin really rejoices in iniquity, and it would freely indulge in it; but always the wages of sin are death, and this the sorrow of the world regrets. As a result, true sorrow over sin is a radical break with all sin; but counterfeit sorrow is a break with certain sins, and that only to the degree that their commitment appears dangerous and harmful for the time being. Godly sorrow, therefore, leads to life and salvation. Or, as the apostle expresses it in II Corinthians 7:10, it "worketh repentance to salvation not to be repented of." But the "sorrow of the world worketh death." The latter really plays with sin. It likes to go the way of sin as far as possible without experiencing the evil consequences of a life of corruption. And the result is always death. But true sorrow over sin is a sure manifestation of conversion. If the prayer of the publican is yours, "God, be merciful to me a sinner," you may be sure that the grace of conversion was wrought in your soul.

The other, or positive, aspect of conversion is the turning to God and to the way of His precepts. This the Bible calls the putting on of the new man in Christ. The apostle writes in Ephesians 4:22-24 that the truth in Jesus is: "That ye put off concerning the former conversation the old man, which is corrupt according to the deceitful lusts; And be renewed in the spirit of your mind; And that ye put on the new

man, which after God is created in righteousness and true holiness."
This new man is the dominion of the new principle of life which the
Holy Spirit instills into your heart when you are reborn. And to put
on this new man signifies the constant endeavor to place yourself and
your whole life under the gracious dominion of that new life. And let
us not make the mistake of imagining that one who thus puts on the
new man now does some great things for Christ, or that he turns the
world upside down, and strives to bring the kingdom of God on earth.
All such high-sounding phrases mean nothing in actual life, are but
idle boasts, and mislead those who are truly converted unto God. But
it does mean that you strive to walk as children of light, and that, too,
in all your earthly life in the midst of the world that lieth in darkness,
in word and deed. You have a delight in the Word of God, so that you
seek and use every opportunity to grow in the knowledge of Jesus
Christ. And you strive to be pleasing to God and to live according to
His precepts. In your personal life, as well as in your family, in the
communion of the church as well as in society, on Sunday but also
during the week, in your office or factory — wherever you are, or
whatever you do, you earnestly endeavor to walk in all good works
before God and men. Thus men will see your good works, and glorify
your Father which is in heaven. And you are willing to endure the
reproach of Christ and in the cause of your Lord not only to believe
on Him but also to suffer with Him, confident that your reward in
heaven is great. Such is true conversion.

You will understand that conversion is a matter that concerns your
whole life as long as you are in this world. Its beginning may be either
very sudden and striking, so that you can point to the place and the
hour when this wonder of grace was first performed upon your soul.
Or it may be gradual and unnoticeable, bound up with the early years
of your childhood, so that you cannot at all remember that you ever
were converted. The former is usually the case with those who live in
ways of gross sin until they have reached the age of maturity. God
suddenly stops them in their pursuit of sin, and turns them radically
about. Paul was so converted on the way to Damascus. The latter
naturally occurs when we are instructed in the truth of the gospel from
infancy, learn to stammer our prayers on mother's lap, and never depart
from the fear of the Lord, but walk in His ways from childhood. And

let me say that the latter is far preferable to the former, and that he who can mention the date and the place of his conversion has nothing to boast because of it. By all means, let him not make of the experience of his sudden conversion a ground of confidence that he is really converted. Often, it seems, this is done. You may frequently hear people boast that they know that they are converted because some ten or twenty years ago they came to Christ. The question is not at all how and when you were converted, nor whether you had an experience of conversion several years in the *past,* but whether you are converted *today.* For whether you were converted suddenly or gradually, as far as the beginning of your conversion is concerned, it surely is only a beginning. It must continue throughout your whole life. It is never finished until you close your eyes forever upon things mundane, your body is laid in the grave, and your soul is with Christ in glory. Nor must we even imagine that conversion gradually becomes less necessary as we grow in grace. The contrary is usually true. Always there is with the Christian the old man, seeking to regain his former dominion; and never does he get rid of the body of this death. And always the new man in Christ must watch and pray and fight the good fight. We must be converted and convert ourselves as long as we live.

This leads us to the final question: is conversion the work of man, or of God in Christ?

The correct answer to this question is this: conversion is that work of God in man whereby the sinner repents and walks in all good works. God converts the sinner, and then the sinner turns. Conversion is, first of all, a gift of grace. He gave repentance to Israel (Acts 5:31); but also to the Gentiles He granted repentance. (Acts 11:18) In Jeremiah 31:18, 19 we read: "Turn thou me, and I shall be turned; for thou art the Lord my God. Surely after that I was turned, I repented; and after that I was instructed, I smote upon my thigh." That expresses the true relation between God's work of conversion and our turning from darkness to light, from sin to righteousness, from the devil to God in Christ. No man is able or willing to convert himself, unless God converts him first. Nor does God's work of conversion leave the sinner inactive, like a "stock and block." In conversion God changes the mind, and the sinner sees all things in a new spiritual light; God turns the will, and the sinner begins to hate sin and long for righteousness;

God works in the heart of the sinner true repentance, and the sinner repents; God draws and the sinner comes; God calls the sinner to turn from his wicked way, by His Word of irresistible grace and power, and the sinner obeys, turns, and finds that God is abundantly merciful. Always God is first in the whole work of salvation, and man's activity is only the fruit of the grace God works in the heart. For we are saved by grace, through faith, and that not of ourselves: it is the gift of God. And the converted sinner will never boast of his work in conversion but give the glory to Him of Whom and through Whom and unto Whom are all things!

He that glorieth, let him glory in the Lord!

Chapter 10

WORKING OUT OUR SALVATION BY GRACE

> . . . work out your own salvation
> with fear and trembling.
> — Philippians 2:12

When God saves us through Jesus Christ our Lord, His purpose is that we may be to the glory of His grace in the Beloved, may declare His praises, and bring forth fruit unto righteousness, walking as children of light in the midst of the world that lieth in darkness. For we are his workmanship, created in Christ Jesus unto good works, which God hath before ordained that we should walk in them. (Ephesians 2:10) Hence, the apostle Paul admonishes the saints in Philippi: "Wherefore, my beloved, as ye have always obeyed, not as in my presence only, but now much more in my absence, work out your own salvation with fear and trembling. For it is God which worketh in you both to will and to do of his good pleasure." (Philippians 2:12, 13)

These words are often thoughtlessly quoted as if, after all, in some sense salvation were of man, not of God. God prepared complete salvation for us; but man must work it out; he must accept it. And whether or not the finished salvation in Christ will actually become his depends upon the choice of his own will. Or, the text is understood and explained as if it teaches a measure of cooperation between God and the sinner who is to be saved. God is willing to save man; but unless man cooperates and puts forth his effort to obtain that salvation, he can never profit by the salvation that is accomplished for him. Not only with respect to his first acceptance of the proffered salvation, but also with a view to its abiding possession, man must cooperate with God in order to be saved. He must work out his own salvation.

However, if we take a little closer look at the text in its context, we soon discover that this cannot be the meaning of the exhortation.

Let us consider, first of all, that the apostle is not addressing these words to unsaved sinners, but to saints in Christ Jesus. To the saints in Philippi he is writing this epistle, and they are those who *are* saved. And he gives them a beautiful testimony. With joy he speaks of their "fellowship in the gospel from the first day even until now." (1:5) He has them in his heart, inasmuch as both in his bonds, and in the defense and confirmation of the gospel, they are all partakers of his grace. (1:7) He prays for them that their love may yet more and more abound unto spiritual discernment, so that they may approve the things that are excellent, may be sincere and without offense till the day of Christ, and be filled with fruits of righteousness, which are by Christ Jesus, unto the glory and praise of God. (1:9-11) They have proved themselves steadfast and faithful, even in the midst of suffering for Christ's sake; and it was given unto them, in the behalf of Christ, not only to believe on Him, but also to suffer for His sake. (1:29) In the immediate context of this admonition to work out their own salvation, the apostle bears them witness that they have always been obedient, not only in his presence, but now much more in his absence. And it is to such saints, to people who are saved through grace, who are strong in the faith, and willing to suffer in the behalf of Christ, to exemplary Christians, that the apostle addresses these words: ". . . work out your own salvation with fear and trembling." Is it, then, not abundantly evident that the meaning of this exhortation cannot possibly be that somehow they must strive to be saved, or must cooperate with God in their salvation?

But the very text ought to be sufficient to warn us against any such interpretation. For notice that the apostle speaks of *their own* salvation, which implies not only that salvation is objectively theirs, but that they have received it: it is already theirs. Nor must we overlook the fact that the apostle exhorts them not to receive salvation, not to work it, not to do anything at all to obtain it, but to work it out, which means that they must let that salvation serve and reach the purpose for which it was given unto them. And, last but not least, the text emphasizes that salvation is of the Lord, even unto the end, so that in working it out they are utterly dependent upon the work of God's grace within them, when there is added as the ground of this exhortation: "For it is God which worketh in you both to will and to do of his good pleasure."

What then does it mean to work out our own salvation?

Salvation, as you know, is the deliverance from all evil, from the guilt and dominion of sin and corruption, and from the power of death, and the being made heirs and partakers of the highest good, namely, eternal righteousness, life, and glory in God's heavenly kingdom through Jesus Christ our Lord, Who was delivered for our transgressions, and raised for our justification. Of this salvation the saints of Philippi and all believers are partakers. They are redeemed by the blood of Christ; they possess the forgiveness of sin; and the imputed and perfect righteousness of God in Christ; they are implanted in the Savior and partake of all His benefits by faith; they are reborn children of God; they are called out of darkness into the marvelous light of God, translated into the kingdom of God's dear Son. That is "their own salvation."

But this salvation they must *work out*. They must let that gift and power of salvation serve the purpose for which it was freely bestowed upon them. They must bring that glorious gift of salvation by grace to manifestation in their whole life. In their entire walk, and that, too, in the midst of the world that lies in darkness, they must reveal themselves as those who have been delivered from the dominion of sin and liberated unto righteousness. From the principle of their new life in Christ Jesus they must live in every walk of life, representing the cause of the Son of God in the world. Thus the salvation that was wrought within them will be worked out by them. In this they are imitators of God, as dear children.

This does not mean that they must now work for the improvement of this present world, which is quite impossible. They need not and they cannot "turn the world upside down." Nor does it mean that they must all be busy in a special sense in the work of the Lord. We do not all have to be preachers or missionaries, or bring souls to Christ, or be elder or deacon in the church, or Sunday-school teacher, in order to cause our salvation to reach its purpose and to reach the end for which it was given unto us. On the contrary, the mother in her home and in the midst of her children, the father in his place of work, whatever it may be, the clerk behind the counter, the cobbler at his bench, every one in his own position and calling, will work out his own salvation when in that calling, and with his whole soul and mind and heart and strength he serves the Lord Christ and lives through faith from the principle of the regenerated life that has been wrought in his inmost heart. To let the light that is within us shine that our Father which is in heaven may be glorified — that it is to work out our own salvation. That this is, indeed, the meaning of this exhortation is evident from what follows it: "Do all things without murmurings and disputings: That ye may be blameless and harmless, the sons of God, without rebuke, in the midst of a crooked and perverse nation, among whom ye shine as lights in the world." (verses 14, 15)

You may, perhaps, remark that there is no need for an exhortation of this kind, seeing that when God works His grace in our hearts, we will naturally and spontaneously work it out and walk in sanctification of life. And there is truth in that statement. But, in the first place, we must always remember that God deals with us as His rational and moral children, and that the working out of our salvation is, therefore, a matter of obedience to His Word. "As obedient children," writes the apostle Peter, "not fashioning yourselves according to the former lusts in your ignorance: But as he which hath called you is holy, so be ye holy in all manner of conversation; Because it is written, Be ye holy; for I am holy." (I Peter 1:14-16) It is Christ Who bears fruit in us when we work out our own salvation, even as the vine bears fruit through the branches; and we have nothing to boast in ourselves. But we bear this fruit, too, with joy and delight, and enjoy the privilege of being His co-workers. Hence, the Word of God treats us as God's free and obedient children and as such addresses us: "Work out your own salvation with fear and trembling."

Besides, let us not forget that as long as we are in this life and in this world, we are in constant need of hearing this word and of being reminded of our calling, of being admonished and encouraged in the good fight of faith. For we must walk as children of light and manifest the salvation of God in the midst of a world that lies in darkness. And that is not easy for the flesh. It will cause us suffering. Even as the world hated Christ, so it will hate us, if we are only faithful in working out our own salvation. For in doing so, we must needs judge the world and condemn its unfruitful works of darkness. And then, let us not forget that we have not attained to the final perfection. We carry the salvation of God in the body of this death. The old man, the sinful flesh, is always present with us. And it is always tempting us, especially when we must suffer the reproach of Christ, rather to hide our own salvation than to work it out, and to compromise and amalgamate ourselves with the evil world. That, in fact, is the great sin of those who are called believers, saints, in our day. We are more and more putting on another yoke with the unbeliever, and it appears as if there is considerable concord between Christ and Belial. Light and darkness seem to merge into the dreary gray of the fog of worldliness, in which no one discerns the direction in which he is going. We are seeking the things below rather than those that are above. We have forgotten the words of the Lord Jesus that he that shall save his life shall lose it, but he that shall lose it shall save it unto life eternal. We are in sore need, therefore, of hearing and heeding the Word of God: "Work out your own salvation with fear and trembling. For it is God that worketh in you both to will and to do of his good pleasure."

This last sentence is added as a ground and reason for the whole admonition, to be sure, but more particularly to explain why we should work out our salvation with *fear and trembling.* You see, these last words do not mean that we must constantly live in fear as to whether we shall ultimately be saved and go to heaven. There are, indeed, Christians who always live in doubt as to their own salvation. They are concerned about their final salvation. They live in constant fear and trembling that they are lost. They cannot surrender themselves with wholehearted confidence to Christ. They never once lift up their heads in the joy of faith to sing songs of redemption to the glory of God's grace in the beloved. Such Christians should honestly examine their own hearts and lives to discover what is wrong, what is the cause of this abnormal and sinful fear and doubt. For, to be sure, Scripture does not approve of such an attitude. And in our admonition the words "fear and trembling" have a rather different meaning. They do not mean that we should be concerned about our final salvation: for we may leave that to God in Christ. He will surely save us, even unto the end. But they do signify that we should be very much concerned about the working out of our own salvation. We should be so deeply impressed with the sacredness of this calling and with the seriousness of this task that we put forth all our efforts, and give it the most pains-taking attention and care. In the fear of God we should tremble at the very thought that, perhaps, we are not working out our own salvation as we ought. Rather than asking the question, which is so frequently asked in our day, how far we dare go into the world, and how closely we can with impunity approach the consuming flame of sin, we should fear and tremble lest we do not keep our garments clean, and lest we do not sufficiently manifest ourselves as children of light. In the true fear of the Lord, with painstaking care, trembling lest you should mar the work, work out your own salvation!

To impress the great importance and deep seriousness of this calling upon us the Scripture adds: "For it is God that worketh in you both to will and to do of his good pleasure."

Here we are, indeed, reminded that salvation is and remains to the very end of the Lord. He works in us through the Spirit of our Lord Jesus Christ. It is He Who gives us the will and the power to walk as children of light. And the text emphasizes that He does so continuous-ly. Salvation, our own salvation, is not to be conceived as something which the Lord once bestows upon us, but which then is ours independ-ently from His indwelling Spirit. On the contrary, it is God Who constantly works in us through the Spirit of the Lord. If that Spirit would leave us but one moment, we would sink back into death. But He never forsakes us. He abides with us for ever. He dwells in us and constantly works within our hearts the will and the power to love and to serve Him with all our heart and mind and soul and strength. It is God Who worketh in you to will and to do. And He does so in the behalf of His own good pleasure, which in the ultimate sense means that the high and only purpose of our salvation is the glory of His grace in the Beloved, even as it has its source in eternal election. Of Him, and through Him, and unto Him is all our salvation!

But as I already said, these last words more particularly express a reason why we should fear and tremble in the working out of our own salvation. To understand this, we must see that all the emphasis falls on the name of God here. Especially in the original this is very clear. We may read the text thus: "For *God* it is that worketh in you. . . ." When you are working out your salvation, you are occupied with the work of *God*. It is of the great and glorious Lord of heaven and earth that your salvation comes. His work it is. To His glory it must tend. Would you not fear and tremble, then, while working out this marvelous work of the great God, lest you make a mistake, lest you think an evil thought, speak a wrong word, commit a sinful act, and lest you do not let your light shine to His glory as brightly as you ought?

Thus the way to final glory is not like taking a Pullman sleeping car and going to sleep till the angels meet us at the final station. It is rather like a steep and rugged road which we can take, on the which we can advance only in the strength of His grace, Who worketh in us to will and to do of His good pleasure. It is a battle. The way often is difficult. The battle is hard. But be of good cheer! The end is sure, the victory is won, the crown of life shall surely be given us in the day of our Lord Jesus Christ, Who fought the battle for us, and Who will fight it through us even unto the end!

Chapter 11

GOOD WORKS THROUGH GRACE

Herein is my Father glorified,
that ye bear much fruit.
— John 15:8

It is the sacred calling of the believer in this world, saved by grace, that he walk in all good works. For "Ye are the light of the world. A city that is set on an hill cannot be hid. Neither do men light a candle, and put it under a bushel, but on a candlestick; and it giveth light to all that are in the house. Let your light so shine before men, that they may see your good works, and glorify your Father which is in heaven." (Matthew 5:14-16) And: "Herein is my Father glorified, that ye bear much fruit; so shall ye be my disciples." (John 15:8) "For we are his workmanship, created in Christ Jesus unto good works, which God hath before ordained that we should walk in them." (Ephesians 2:10)

Especially this last passage is significant in this connection. For it emphasizes the truth that we are saved by grace even to the very end. As believers we are God's workmanship, in no sense our own. It is He that created us, made us new creatures in Christ Jesus by His almighty power of wondrous grace. And He performed this wonder of grace in order, to be sure, that we should do good works; but even these works were ordained for every one of us before the foundation of the world by God Himself, and it is our privilege to walk in them. To elucidate this last truth, we may use the illustration of a great chorus rendering Handel's *Messiah*. If such a rendering is to be successful, every member of the chorus and each voice, tenor and bass, soprano and alto, as well as the soloists, the orchestra, and the accompanist at the organ, must know and perform his part so as to blend into the grand harmony and beauty of the whole. But in order to attain to this end they must strictly follow their music. For the whole of the performance by the chorus, as well as the several parts, have been "before ordained" by the artist who composed the oratorio; and the members of the chorus only "walk in" the parts that have thus been ordained for them. This may be applied to the good works of all the saints in Christ. The church of Christ is not a mere number of saved believers: it is a body, a unity. And its purpose is to show forth the glory of God in Christ. This one theme all the saints sing and develop in their good works, each in his own position and performing his own part. And the great Artist ordained and prepared all the several parts of this glorious theme for every one of the saints, just as He by grace prepared them all for the parts they are to perform. He created us in Christ Jesus exactly unto those good works which He prepared for us, that we might walk in them.

From this statement of Holy Writ we wish to elicit a few truths concerning the nature and purpose of good works.

What are good works?

First of all, we may remark that as far as their material is concerned, good works are those that are in accord with the will of God as revealed unto us in Scripture. In doing good works we must "prove what is that good, and acceptable, and perfect will of God." (Romans 12:2) God alone is good; and His will is good; and He alone has the prerogative and is able to determine what is good. Good works, therefore, are first of all characterized by unconditional and unquestioning obedience to the will of God. When God speaks, we are silent: we just listen. When He commands, we obey without murmuring, without objection, and without reservations. This means that we never assume the authority to determine for ourselves what shall be called good. It was exactly the sin of our first parents that they presumed to settle the question as to good and evil for themselves. It implies, too, that the utility principle may not and cannot possibly determine what is good or evil. This is frequently done by the unbelieving world. The question is asked whether a certain action or course of action or law or institution of man *works*, or whether it pays. If it does, regardless of the question whether it is according to the will and law of God, it is simply adopted and followed. The result is, of course, ultimate destruction. A glaring example of this method of determining what is good is found in the way the divorce problem is solved in the courts of our land. Sinful man, rather than submitting himself to the law of God, by his darkened understanding judges what is expedient for him, tramples under foot the precepts of the Most High, and works out his own destruction. Nor dare one appeal to his good intentions to decide that an act that in itself was contrary to the law of God is good. It may seem possible to a simple man to tell a lie with the best of intentions, but that does not justify the lie. Good works are those, and those only, that are strictly in harmony with the will of God as revealed unto us in His Word.

But this leads us to another, equally important question. It may be put in this way: what does it mean that our actions must be in harmony with the will or law of God in order to be good? Is any deed as such, an act of man as we observe him, as it appears to us, supposing that it is completely and perfectly in harmony with the will of God, necessarily a good work? Suppose that a man offers prayer in public and that the contents of his prayer are in accord with the will of God, does it follow that he performs a good work? Or suppose that he is a preacher and that he proclaims the gospel and the full counsel of God according to the Scriptures, does that outward act of preaching necessarily constitute a good work? Or say that a church member drops a thousand dollars in the collection plate for the cause of charity, or of missions, or for some other good cause, is that outward act sufficient to determine that it is good before God and that it is perfectly in harmony with His holy will?

The answer to this question must be an emphatic negative. And the reason for this is twofold.

First of all, we must not forget that the outward act, the deed as it is seen by men, is but a part, and that, too, a very small part, of the entire deed as it is witnessed by the living God. When you see a man drop a thousand dollars in the collection plate, you observe but the outward act. There is back of that hand that drops the gift the mind of the giver that contemplated it, the desire that motivated the act, the will that finally determined upon the act. And back of the mind and will and desire of the giver there is the deep heart of man, whence are all the issues of life. Before he drops his money in the plate, the man has been thinking about it; and that, too, belongs to the deed he performs. He has been desiring something. He placed before his mind a certain objective, a purpose that he wished to attain; and by this he was motivated, urged to perform the act of giving the money. His whole inner man was in action before he ever dropped the money in the collection plate, and all this inner action belongs very really to the deed itself in the sight of God.

Secondly, we must consider that the will or revealed law of God concerning our life and walk does not merely cover the outward activity of man, but also his inner life, his mind and will and all his desires. O, the matter were not so serious and difficult if the law of God were satisfied with the outward appearance of the deed before men, so that it would call a man's work good if only he conforms himself in his external deportment to God's will, does not swear and curse, commit adultery and steal, murder and slander, goes to church on Sunday and observes the sabbath, sings and prays and gives alms. But the law of God is this: "Thou shalt love the Lord thy God with all thy heart, and with all thy mind, and with all thy soul, and with all thy strength." And that throws a different light upon the question of good works. The law is a law of love. It demands that we shall be motivated by the love of God in all our actions. It covers not only the outward appearance of the deed but also the hidden part that is in the mind, the will, the desires, that has its origin in the heart of man. It demands that a work shall be good and perfect in the sight of God from its deepest root in the heart to its ripened fruit in the external act. And unless a work of man is in full accord with that law of the love of God from its first contemplation, yea, from its hidden origin in the heart, to the outward deed, it is evil in the sight of God and may be very abominable to Him indeed, no matter how it may appear to us. The very sacrifice of the wicked is an abomination to Jehovah! (Proverbs 15:8)

This brings us to the question of purpose and motive. The purpose of good works is the glory of God, the manifestation of the beauty of His grace in the Beloved. "Let your light so shine before men, that they may see your good works, and glorify your Father which is in heaven." (Matthew 5:16) If our works are to be good in the sight of God, they must be motivated by the will and desire to attain to that purpose. Purpose and motive are closely related. Purpose denotes the end which we have in view in performing a certain deed; and motive is the will, the urge, and the desire that spurs us on from within to seek that end. Now God's purpose is His own glory. And that purpose must be ours if our works are to be good in His sight. Good works, therefore, are motivated by the will and desire to reach that purpose, to glorify our Father which is in heaven. Hence, in order to determine whether or not a certain act on our part is good, we must not merely ask *what* we did, but also *why* we performed it, and what was the purpose we had in view.

Let us consider a few illustrations to make this plain. Suppose you are an honest business man, and in all your dealings you treat your customers fairly. The question arises: why are you honest in your dealings? If your answer is that you love the Lord your God with all your heart, and that it is your desire to serve and promote the glory of your God even in your business, all is well. Your honest dealing is a good work, indeed. But suppose that, upon honest and thorough self-examination you come to the conclusion that your honest dealing is merely motivated by the desire to establish and maintain a good business, by the realization that honesty pays: your reward is then gone. You are in your deepest heart seeking self, a good business, worldly gain. You are not seeking God's glory, but carnal gain; and you are motivated by covetousness. In that respect you are no different from and no better than the man of dishonest dealings who is motivated by the same desire for profit. All that is not to the glory of God is sin!

A striking example of this apparent good work that is evil in the sight of the Lord is the Pharisee of Jesus' day. He was scrupulously religious. It was his constant effort to bring his external life in harmony with the law in its minutest details. He fasted and prayed and gave alms and observed the sabbath blamelessly. He went to the temple and offered his sacrifices and paid his vows. In the sight of men he was a perfect example of piety, and his good works were numerous. But if that same Pharisee had taken the trouble to make a little introspection and to examine himself from the viewpoint of the question, "Why dost thou stand here on the street corner to pray and to give alms and to perform all thy good works?" he would have come to the discovery that he was seeking the honor of men, not the glory of God. His purpose was his own glory. His motive was stinking pride. He was an abomination in the sight of God. All his praying and sacrificing and giving alms was, in the sight of God, by no means less abominable than the act of the highway robber and murderer who openly commits his crimes. And the Lord does not hesitate to compare this pious Pharisee to a whitewashed sepulchre, beautiful without, but within full of dead men's bones and uncleanness.

A similar example you may find in Jehu of Old Testament days. He received a special command of God to exterminate the house of Ahab for their wickedness. And he zealously and thoroughly obeyed the Lord and did his work well. Yet, although he was so zealous in obeying the Lord as far as the outward deed was concerned, he himself never departed from the ways of Jeroboam who caused Israel to sin; and in the prophecy of Hosea we read that the house of Jehu is punished by the Lord for the blood which they shed in exterminating the house of Ahab. But how is this possible? The answer is simply this: although outwardly Jehu was perfectly obedient to this special command of the Lord, his inner motive was corrupt. He sought his own glory and the realization of his own ambition to ascend the throne of Israel, rather than the glory of Jehovah!

And so you see that a man may perform an outwardly good act from a very wicked motive. Nor dare we say that these outwardly beautiful works that are inwardly corrupt are due to an operation of grace by the Holy Spirit. The Holy Spirit does not attach good fruit to a corrupt tree, nor does He call such fruit good. Either the tree is good and its fruit is good, or the tree is corrupt and its fruit is also corrupt, no matter how beautiful it may appear to the eye of man. When the Holy Spirit takes hold of a man, He does not polish his outward appearance; but He takes hold of his inmost heart, regenerates him, makes him a new creature in Christ Jesus, unites him through faith with Christ, and remains in him to dwell in him, to sanctify him, to fill him with the grace of the Lord Jesus. For we are His workmanship, created in Christ Jesus unto good works, which God before ordained that we should walk in them. This is the reason why the root of all good works is faith in the Lord Jesus Christ. All that is not of faith is sin. (Romans 14:23) For by faith we are in Christ Jesus, one plant with Him, so that we live out of Him, or rather, so that He lives in us. And as the vine bears its fruit in the branches, so the Lord Jesus Christ bears the fruit of His grace in all His saints. For we are saved by grace, through faith, and that not of ourselves: it is the gift of God!

What, then, shall be our conclusion?

First of all, no doubt, in the light of the Scriptural doctrine concerning good works, we shall all have to acknowledge in deep humility that we are still far from complete perfection. Even our best works are defiled with sin, and we have but a small beginning of the new obedience. Daily we have need to seek our refuge in the shadow of the cross and to wash our garments by faith in the blood of the Lamb, that we may obtain the forgiveness of sins. And, secondly, we have nothing to boast, not even on the basis of the best of our good works. For they are all of grace. They are not gifts of ours to God, but they are gifts of God to us: works in which we may walk, and by walking in which we are blessed indeed!

He that glorieth, let him glory in the Lord!

Chapter 12

SUFFERING THROUGH GRACE

> For unto you it is given in the behalf of Christ, not only to believe on him, but also to suffer for his sake.
>
> — Philippians 1:29

For every man suffering is an unpleasant experience. It is an evil which we try to avoid, an enemy which we dread and from which we try to escape, or from whose clutches we desperately struggle to liberate ourselves. Suffering is something which we naturally dislike, whatever form it may assume, whether that of bodily pain and agony, or of grief and sorrow of soul, or of shame and reproach of our person. If it is cowardice to shrink from suffering in itself, when no other and higher interest demands it, no nobler motive prompts us to choose it, all men are cowards. To like suffering is a contradiction in terms. And in the state of final perfection, in the new creation, when God's tabernacle shall be with men, all sorrow and crying shall flee away forever, and God shall wipe away all tears from our eyes.

Yet in certain circumstances, under certain conditions, suffering is very definitely to be preferred and to be chosen deliberately. This is true even with respect to certain natural and earthly conditions and relations which may arise in human life. A father will fly in the face of danger and death and throw himself into the smoke and flame of his burning house when he discovers that one of his children was left behind in the fire. A mother will protect her darling with her own body against an enemy far more powerful than she. A government may, under certain conditions, prefer all the agonies of war to the enjoyment of peace. But this is always and supremely true when suffering must be endured for righteousness' sake. It is immeasurably better and preferable to suffer and remain on the side of righteousness, Christ, God, than to avoid suffering by denying the name of our Lord and choosing for ourselves the way of the flesh and of the world. When we face the alternative of an ethical, spiritual evil or suffering for righteousness' sake, it is infinitely to be preferred to choose the latter than to commit the former.

This truth is strongly emphasized in Scripture by precept and example.

On the one hand, they who are saved by grace and work out their own salvation in this world are warned that they must expect suffering with Christ and for His sake. The Lord Jesus declares that "If any man will come after me, let him deny himself, and take up his cross, and follow me." (Matthew 16:24) "And he that taketh not his cross, and followeth after me is not worthy of me. He that findeth his life shall lose it: and he that loseth his life for my sake shall find it." (Matthew 10:38, 39) He warns His disciples that the days will come when they shall deliver them up to be afflicted, and shall kill them; and they shall be hated of all nations for His name's sake. (Matthew 24:9) And He explains to them that if they were of the world, the world would love its own; but because they are not of the world, but He has chosen them out of the world, therefore the world hates them. But they must remember that it hated Him before it hated them. (John 15:18, 19) And the time will even come that "whosoever killeth you will think that he doeth God service." (John 16:2) And in this suffering for Christ's sake all the saints that have gone before are our examples. For they had "trial of cruel mockings and scourgings, yea, moreover of bonds and imprisonment: They were stoned, they were sawn asunder, were tempted, were slain with the sword; they wandered about in sheepskins and goatskins; being destitute, afflicted, tormented; (Of whom the world was not worthy:) they wandered in deserts, and in mountains, and in dens and caves of the earth." (Hebrews 11:36-38)

On the other hand, Scripture emphasizes everywhere that the believer must always prefer suffering to fellowship with the unfruitful works of darkness, and that in his very suffering he has abundant reasons to rejoice. "We glory in tribulations also," the apostle writes in Romans 5:3. "My brethren, count it all joy when you fall into diverse temptations," James exhorts us. (James 1:2) "If ye be re-proached for the name of Christ, happy are ye: for the spirit of glory and of God resteth upon you: on their part he is evil spoken of, but on your part he is glorified." (I Peter 4:14) And the Lord Jesus teaches us: "Blessed are they which are persecuted for righteousness' sake: for their's is the kingdom of heaven. Blessed are ye, when men shall revile you, and persecute you, and shall say all manner of evil against you falsely, for my sake." (Matthew 5:10, 11) And so the Scriptures admonish us that we should be faithful even unto death, that we may obtain the crown of life. (Revelation 2:10)

Now also this blessing and spiritual virtue, whereby we discern and choose suffering for Christ's sake as something preferable to freedom from suffering in the way of unrighteousness, is a gift of grace. For so the apostle writes to the church of Philippi and to the believers of all ages: "For unto you it is given in the behalf of Christ, not only to be-lieve on him, but also to suffer for his sake." (Philippians 1:29) It is given us — and in the original we read "it is given you by grace" — in the behalf of Christ to suffer for His sake.

Let us consider this marvelous gift of grace a little more closely.

What does it mean to suffer in the behalf of Christ and for His sake? We may notice that in the immediate context of the text in Philippians the apostle admonished the believers that they should walk as it "be-cometh the gospel of Christ," that they should stand fast in one spirit, and thus should strive together for the gospel of Christ. Briefly, this means that they must walk as children of light in the midst of the world, united unto the one purpose to maintain, proclaim, testify of the gospel of Christ, and manifest the beauty and grace of that gospel in their whole life. At the same time, the apostle had suggested that if they so walked and contended for the faith of the gospel, there would be adversaries who would oppose them and cause them to suffer. But they must not be terrified on their account: for this persecution and opposition is to the enemy a sure token of perdition, but to the believer a testimony of God, a sign of salvation. For it is given to him of grace in the behalf of Christ to suffer for His sake.

To suffer in the behalf of Christ, therefore, means, first of all, to suffer because of Him and because of all that He represents. Christ has a cause in this world. It is the cause of the kingdom of God, the cause of God's covenant, His Name, His glory, His righteousness. That cause of God must be represented. When Christ Himself was in the world, He contended for this cause in person; and the world hated Him and opposed Him and caused Him to suffer exactly because He strove for and represented the cause of God, of His righteousness and truth. Now Christ is no more personally in this world. He was crucified and was raised from the dead, and is exalted to the highest glory at the right hand of God. However, He is very really in His church, in His saints, in whom He dwells by His Spirit and whom He calls and instructs through His Word. Through them He still represents and contends for the cause of God in the world. He becomes manifest in and through them. And so, by His grace, believers represent the cause of Christ. And if you suffer in the behalf of Christ and for His sake, it is this fact, that Christ becomes revealed in you, in your walk and confession in this world, that is the occasion of your suffering. You suffer literally because of the Person of Christ. It is Christ Who is hated by the world. It is Christ Whom they want to kill with their reproach. They really want to kill Christ and empty the vials of their hatred over His head. And since they cannot reach Him personally any more, seeing that He is in glory, they hate and persecute those who represent Him, in whom He becomes manifest in the world.

But, secondly, to suffer in the behalf of Christ also implies the idea of suffering for the advantage and benefit of Christ. Christ must be revealed. His name may not remain hid but must be made manifest. The glory and beauty of His power and grace must be fully shown forth and declared in all the world, and that, not only in order that His church may be gathered and His kingdom may be extended, but also that the world may be condemned and the unfruitful works of darkness may be rebuked. This cause believers must serve. And to serve this cause they must suffer, in order that the measure of iniquity may be filled, sin may become fully manifest as enmity against God, and the evil world may become ripe for the day of the revelation of the righteous judgment of God. Because of Christ, but also in the interest of the cause of Christ, it is given to the saints in this world to suffer for His sake.

Now in order to understand how Scripture can speak of this suffering as a gift of grace, we must note that it is voluntary. It is a form of suffering which under certain conditions believers deliberately choose. This is not true of the suffering of this present time in general. When sickness attacks your frame, or when sorrow and death enter your home, you have no choice. This kind of suffering is simply inflicted upon you without your will. You cannot avoid or escape it. But in regard to the suffering in the behalf of Christ this is different. You are placed before an alternative, and you must make a choice. The alternative is always suffering with Christ, or freedom from that suffering with Belial; the reproach of Christ, or the pleasures of the world; fellowship with Christ in His death, or fellowship with the world in its life. And he who suffers in the behalf of Christ makes a decision. He considers the alternatives and evaluates them in order to determine what is preferable. And he reaches the conclusion that the reproach of Christ is to be esteemed far greater riches than the treasures of Egypt, that it is far preferable to die with Christ than to live with Belial. And having reached this conclusion, he follows it up to the very end: he deliberately chooses to suffer with Christ, and without hesitation he rejects the proffered deliverance that is presented to him on condition that he will deny Christ and walk in the way of the world.

It is thus that the prophets and apostles and all the Bible saints suffered. They were "tortured, not accepting deliverance." (Hebrews 11:35) It was thus that the martyrs of the early church chose to suffer with Christ. They were placed before the alternative of being dumped alive into a seething caldron of boiling oil, or making a bow as a sign of worship to Caesar. And it was often made extremely easy for them, so easy that in our day we would probably discover a thousand reasons why we would be allowed to choose the latter. They were permitted to maintain their confession that Christ is Lord, if only by a slight bow to the image of Caesar they would admit that the Roman emperor was also Lord. But in the behalf of Christ they deliberately chose the awful death of the seething caldron, not accepting deliverance, insisting that Christ is the Lord alone! It is thus that the martyrs of the Reformation preferred the reproa of Christ. The instruments of horrible torture to which they were subjected by the Spanish Inquisition may still be seen in some parts of the old world, where they have been preserved as a silent testimony of the faith of these faithful witnesses. They were stretched on the rack, and placed before the choice of

renouncing their faith or being torn apart limb by limb. But they preferred the latter, not accepting deliverance. And so, the saints have
been cast into dungeons, have been killed by the sword, burned at the
stake, thrown before the wild beasts, and become the offscouring of
the world because of the witness of God and the faith of the gospel.

And how about us? This form of persecution does not exist in our
land, though in other lands thousands have suffered and do suffer for
Christ's sake even today. But even though the laws of our own country
do not permit such cruel forms of persecution, is therefore the Word of
the Lord Jesus no longer true, that they shall hate us even as they hated
Him? Must not also today the faithful, who do not hide their light and
who refuse to have fellowship with the unfruitful works of darkness
and to put on another yoke with the unbeliever, suffer reproach,
mockery, and shame? Are we, too, not frequently confronted with the
alternative of suffering the loss of position and name, of a job and our
business, unless we will deny our faith and become amalgamated with
the ungodly world? And what is our choice? Listen! The choice of
him who lives by grace is to suffer in the behalf of Christ! To choose
the world, its name and glory, its treasures and pleasures, our job and
position, even our life, is, to say the least, not to live by grace. For it
is given you of grace, not only to believe in Him, but also to suffer for
His sake!

Yes, indeed, only through the power of God's marvelous grace in
Christ Jesus, that redeemed us from sin, that delivered us from the
dominion of corruption, that translated us out of darkness into His
marvelous light, and that is still working within us to will and to do of
His good pleasure, can this choice be made. By nature we will always
choose the world, our present life, our name and job and earthly
prosperity. The natural man cannot possibly understand that the reproach of Christ must be esteemed greater riches than the treasures of
the world. How could he? He is without God in the world, and with
this world all his life is bound up. For, first of all, by grace it is given
us to believe in Christ. And believing in Him, by that faith we live out
of Him, and He lives in us. And living out of Him, we are new creatures.
We have a radically new way of judging and evaluating things, so that
we consider that the statutes of the Lord are more to be desired than
much fine gold, and consider all things but dross for the excellency of

Christ Jesus our Lord. In that light we do, indeed, discern that it is far better to lose the whole world than to be unfaithful to our Lord. But, secondly, through that grace we also look forward to a better resurrection and know that if here we suffer with Christ, we shall also be glorified with Him.

To suffer with Christ is a great blessing. For, first of all, the very consciousness that we are deemed worthy, together with all the saints, to suffer in His behalf and for righteousness' sake, affords us unspeakable joy and profound peace. Secondly, there is a present fruit which is reaped in the way of this suffering: for tribulation worketh patience, and patience the approved state, and the approved state hope: and hope maketh not ashamed! (Romans 5:3-5) Finally, there is at the end of this road of suffering for Christ's sake — and mark you well: at the end of no other road — the crown of life, the glory with Christ! And the sufferings of this present time are not worthy to be compared with that glory.

Rejoice, and be exceeding glad: for great is your reward in heaven!

Chapter 13

VICTORY THROUGH GRACE

> ...be thou faithful unto death,
> and I will give thee a crown of life.
> — Revelation 2:10

The promise of final salvation and glory in the kingdom of heaven is for those who gain the victory in the battle of faith.

Repeatedly we read in the letter of Christ to the seven churches of Asia, preserved for us in the second and third chapters of the Book of Revelation, that the Lord will realize His promise to him that overcometh. "To him that overcometh will I give to eat of the tree of life, which is in the midst of the paradise of God." (Revelation 2:7) To him that overcometh Christ will give a crown of life. (2:10) He will give him to eat of the hidden manna, and give him a white stone, and in the stone a new name written, which no man knoweth saving he that receiveth it. (2:17) He will give him power over the nations, even as Christ received of His Father, and the morning star. (2:26-28) He shall be clothed with white raiment; and his name shall not be blotted out of the book of life, and Christ will confess his name before His Father and before the holy angels. (3:5) He shall be made a pillar in the temple of God, so that he shall no more go out thence, and a new name, the name of God, and the name of the heavenly Jerusalem, and the new name of Christ, will be written upon him. (3:12) And it shall be granted to him to sit with Christ in His throne, even as Christ also overcame, and is set down with His Father in His throne. (3:21) Indeed, only he that overcometh shall inherit all things. (Revelation 21:7) And he that endureth unto the end shall be saved. (Matthew 10:22)

All this presupposes, of course, that the believer in this world has a battle to fight, and that only in the way of battle can he gain the victory and obtain the crown. And so, everywhere the Scriptures exhort God's people to fight that battle. They must put on the whole armor of God, that they may be able to stand against the wiles of the devil. For they wrestle not against flesh and blood, but against principalities, against powers, against the rulers of the darkness of this world, against spiritual wickednesses in high places; and they need the whole armor of God, that they may be able to withstand in the evil day, and having done all, to stand. (Ephesians 6:11-17) By Paul's word to Timothy we are exhorted to fight the good fight of faith and to lay hold on eternal life. (I Timothy 6:12) Paul himself testifies: "I have fought the good fight, I have finished my course, I have kept the faith." (II Timothy 4:7) The believer is exhorted to run with patience the race that is set before him, laying aside every encumbrance, and the sin that so easily besets him, looking unto Jesus, the Author and Finisher of our faith, Who for the joy that was set before Him endured the cross, despising the shame, and is set down at the right hand of the throne of God. (Hebrews 12:1, 2) And the church must hold fast that which she has, that no one take her crown. (Revelation 3:11)

In this spiritual battle the Christian occupies a very precarious position — in fact, an apparently impossible and hopeless one. Everything that is of this world is against him. He is against himself. For although it is true that he is a new creature, God's workmanship created in Christ Jesus unto good works, he is renewed only in principle, and his whole nature stands in diametric opposition to the new principle of life which he received in regeneration and from which he lives by faith. He has but a small beginning of the new obedience; and the motions of sin that are in his members make it quite impossible for him, as long as he is in this life, to live without sin.

I am well aware of the fact that there are those who deny this and who claim that the Christian in this world can live a perfect life. And sometimes you can hear them make the claim that for a certain period — for a week, for a month, for a whole year, perhaps — they lived sinlessly. And they appeal to such passages as I John 3:9, which declare that one who is born of God cannot sin, because His seed remains in him, and he cannot sin, because he is born of God. But, first of all, let me appeal to your own experience as a Christian: upon some candid introspection must we not all confess that this ideal of perfectionism was never and can never be attained by us in this life? O, as long as we stay on the surface and merely consider our external life and conversation, we may, perhaps, flatter ourselves that we are rather far advanced on the road to perfection. But as soon as we dig down below the surface and investigate our inner life, our thoughts and desires, our inclinations and secret longings, there is nothing left of this proud boast. Secondly, passages like that quoted from I John 3:9 do not teach us that it is *merely possible* for him that is born of God to live without sin, but that it is *impossible* for him to sin. He that is born of God *cannot* sin! He is not like Adam in the original state of righteousness, who was free to obey his God but could also fall away from Him. He has attained to the state of highest freedom: he can sin no more! And that is true of the Christian as far as the inner principle of the new life is concerned that was implanted in him. But it is not true of his nature. In regeneration he does not receive a new body nor another soul. He lives the life of Christ in his old nature. And that old nature is opposed to that new life. The new life is holy, the old nature is sinful. The new life is heavenly, the old nature is earthy.

That is why, in the third place, the Word of God everywhere teaches us that the believer has a fight against himself. "If we say that we have no sin, we deceive ourselves, and the truth is not in us." (I John 1:8) What Christian does not from experience heartily agree with the Word of God in Romans 7, where the apostle Paul describes his own battle in the following words: "For that which I do I allow not: for what I would, that do I not; but what I hate, that do I. If then I do that which I would not, I consent unto the law that it is good. Now then it is no more I that do it, but sin that dwelleth in me. For I know that in me (that is, in my flesh,) dwelleth no good thing: for to will is present with me; but how to perform that which is good I find not. For the good that I would I do not: but the evil which I would not, that I do. Now if I do that I would not, it is no more I that do it, but sin that dwelleth in me.... O wretched man that I am! who shall deliver me from the body of this death? I thank God through Jesus Christ our Lord." (vss. 15-20, 24, 25) Indeed, in the battle which the Christian must fight to gain the victory he is against himself: the foe is within the gates!

Add to this that all that is in the world agrees and cooperates with that old nature, that foe within the gates, and conspires to overcome the new man in the believer. Add, too, that the devil and his mysterious and powerful hosts of spiritual wickednesses in high places concentrate all their power upon him to his defeat and destruction. Is it then not evident that his position is indeed a very precarious one? There is nothing in all the world to help him, to sustain him in the fight, to encourage him in battle. Literally everything is against him. For the world is full of the lust of the flesh and the lust of the eyes and the pride of life; and through it all it appeals strongly to his old nature. It would confuse and lead him astray from the path of the truth by its false philosophy. It would seduce him by the siren's song of its treasures and pleasures, its honor and glory, its "abundant life." It would frighten him into submission and apostasy and unfaithfulness to the cause of Christ by its hatred and fury, its threats and persecution. And the devil goeth about as a roaring lion, seeking whom he may devour! Compare with these mighty powers the small principle of the new life and obedience which the believer has in his heart, and you will agree that God places His child in the world in an éxtremely dangerous, an apparently impossible position. It would appear that he could never survive, let alone gain the victory and attain to the promised salvation.

Will he, then, be able to stand and to persevere even unto the end? And if so, how?

To this question all who profess to believe in salvation by divine grace reply with one accord: yes, he will be able, but only through preserving grace. The same marvelous grace that was revealed in the cross of God's only begotten Son, and that was bestowed upon us by the Spirit of Christ, that raised us from the dead and called us out of darkness into the marvelous light of God, is the power which must keep us, strengthen us, constantly sanctify us, enlighten us, and cause us to discern spiritual things, if we are to stand and gain the victory in this humanly impossible battle of faith. Fighting in our own strength, we must surely be defeated. Standing in our own power, we will surely fall. Depending on our own wisdom, we will surely be entangled in the snare of temptation. Boasting of our own faithfulness, we will, as Peter of old, surely deny Him. We are saved by grace. That means also that we are preserved by grace. Without Christ we can do nothing. And if any man thinketh he standeth, let him beware lest he fall! Not one step on the way of sanctification can we take without His grace. About this there is no dispute. Every Christian knows that he is strong only when he is weak, and that God's strength is made perfect in his weakness. We persevere and overcome only through the marvelous power of God's preserving grace.

Yet, even so, we must say more than this if we would really confess that we are saved by grace only, and that this grace of God is absolutely sovereign. For it is indeed possible to confess all this, to ascribe our preservation entirely to God's grace, and yet, in the end, to turn about and present the whole matter of our preservation as ultimately dependent upon man, upon the believer himself. A striking illustration of this is offered by the last of the five articles which were composed by the Arminians in 1610. In the strongest language they there confess that after the believer is saved, regenerated, and called, he still can do absolutely nothing of himself, and that he cannot even so much as think anything good or will anything that is pleasing in the sight of God. Utterly dependent he is upon the grace of God to preserve him. But the end of that article overthrows this whole declaration concerning the indispensableness of God's grace to persevere, when they suggest that a man may make himself unworthy of this grace and that, therefore, it cannot be maintained as certain that the believer will never fall away finally and completely, so that he attains to the final salvation and glory in the heavenly kingdom.

You see, the important and fundamental question, the answer to which decides whether or not a man really believes and confesses wholeheartedly that salvation is by sovereign grace, is always this: who determines the salvation of man? Who is first: God or man? Must man first open his heart, or, at least, be willing to receive Christ, before God can save him? If your answer to this question is in the affirmative, you may extol the grace of God that saves us as loudly and highly as you wish, but you deny the truth of sovereign grace nevertheless. You make God dependent on man, you present the grace of God as contingent upon the will of the creature. And if this is the relation between grace and the will of man in the beginning, when a man first comes to Christ, it must needs remain such even to the end. Then you will say, to be sure, that the believer is preserved by grace and that he can do nothing of himself; but you will always add that he must will to receive this grace and that it is always possible for him to reject the grace He wants accepted, and thus to fall away into perdition. God's almighty hand is strong to save and to preserve you unto the end; but if you must hold on to that hand, your preservation after all depends upon the puny strength of your hand, not upon the omnipotent power of His hand.

But thanks be to God, Who giveth us the victory through our Lord Jesus Christ! His grace is free and absolutely sovereign. It is rooted in eternal election. It is forever based on the perfect sacrifice of Jesus Christ our Lord. It sovereignly and irresistibly takes hold of us, making us new creatures in Christ, and that, too, not because we will, but in spite of the fact that we do not will, and cannot possibly will to come to Him before His grace has touched us; not because we seek Him first, but because He seeks us; not because we love Him, but while we are yet enemies. Grace must needs be first if it is to save man who is dead through trespasses and sins. And first it is, always first, first from beginning to end. It is first in regenerating us, it is first in calling us, it is first in drawing us to Christ, it is first in bestowing upon us the gift of faith. And it is also first in preserving us unto the end. He preserves us; and because He preserves, we persevere. It is He that worketh within us to will and to do of His good pleasure — yes, indeed, also to will; and then we work out our own salvation. That is the meaning of salvation by grace. He that glorieth, let him glory in the Lord!

And that is the reason why the believer can never perish. "For the gifts and calling of God are without repentance." (Romans 11:29) "All that the Father giveth me shall come to me: and him that cometh to me I will in no wise cast out. For I came down from heaven not to do mine own will, but the will of him that sent me. And this is the Father's will which hath sent me, that of all that he hath given me I should lose nothing, but should raise it up again at the last day." (John 6:37-39) And again, "And I give unto them eternal life; and they shall never perish, neither shall any man pluck them out of my hand." (John 10:28) And so we are "persuaded, that neither death, nor life, nor angels, nor principalities, nor powers, nor things present, nor things to come, Nor height, nor depth, nor any other creature, shall be able to separate us from the love of God, which is in Christ Jesus our Lord." (Romans 8:38, 39)

Do not object that this gospel makes men "careless and profane," so that they become utterly passive, seeing that God must do it all anyway, and that we will surely have the victory, whether we fight the good fight of faith or not. For the sovereign grace of God does not enervate man, but strengthens him and steels him to fight. It does not make man passive, but active. It does not make us profane, but it sanctifies us. It fills us with the love of God, so that we gladly receive and heed and obey His Word, and put on the whole armor of God, that we may be able to withstand in the evil day. The assurance that the victory is ours does not make us sit down passively but causes us to be strong and courageous in the battle.

"Therefore, my beloved brethren, be ye stedfast, unmoveable, always abounding in the work of the Lord, forasmuch as ye know that your labour is not in vain in the Lord." (I Corinthains 15:58)

Chapter 14

ASSURANCE OF GRACE

> ... give diligence to make your
> calling and election sure.
> — II Peter 1:10

The Word of God in II Peter 1:10 admonishes believers to make their calling and election sure. In fact, it exhorts them to give diligence to do so. And it emphasizes the importance of this spiritual diligence on the part of believers by adding, first, that doing this they shall never stumble, and, secondly, that thus the entrance into the eternal kingdom of our Lord Jesus Christ shall be richly supplied unto them.

It is evident, then, that we have something to do with election. There are those who would deny this. They do not deny the truth of this doctrine. On the contrary, they understand very well that the Word of God teaches it; and they profess to believe that God has chosen those who are to be saved from before the foundation of the world. But to them it is a very impracticable doctrine. It is a mystery. It belongs to those things that are hid from us, that are for the Lord our God, not for us. The less we think about it, the better for us. And by all means it should not be preached, except occasionally to remind us that there is such a truth. Above all, we should never ask ourselves the question whether we are of God's elect, lest we become confused. Our calling is to preach and to believe the gospel, to accept Jesus Christ, and to leave the deep things to God.

However, this may all be very well for those who are doctrinally lazy and ignorant, who are satisfied with a gospel they can write on their thumbnail; for him who has his delight in the truth of God's Word, who is founded in the truth of the whole counsel of God, such an attitude can never be satisfactory. Why should the Holy Scriptures so frequently speak of this truth if it were not the purpose of God that we should be instructed in it? And how dare we claim that we have nothing to do with it, and that it is an impracticable doctrine, if the Bible exhorts us that we shall make our calling and election sure, and that we shall give diligence to do this? Surely, this exhortation places us before the question: how can we do this? What can we do to make our calling and election sure? And before we can even begin to answer this, we must determine the meaning of this exhortation.

Election is the eternal fountain head of grace and salvation. It is the eternal good pleasure of God according to which, for His own name's sake and with absolute sovereignty, He chose out of the whole human race a church ordained unto eternal life and glory. It is not based on any foreseen goodness or faith in man, as if some were better or more willing than others: for then the elect would have something whereof to boast in themselves. On the contrary, election is sovereign and free. It downs all man's pride. And it means that God is the Lord also in the matter of salvation. And this truth is not based on a few isolated passages of Holy Scripture, but is so taught throughout the Bible that it is presented as the foundation of our faith. For the God and Father of our Lord Jesus Christ "hath blessed us with all spiritual blessings in heavenly places in Christ: According as he hath chosen us in him before the foundation of the world, that we should be holy and without blame before him in love." (Ephesians 1:3, 4) And He has "predestinated us unto the adoption of children by Jesus Christ to himself, according to the good pleasure of his will, To the praise of the glory of his grace, wherein he hath made us accepted in the beloved." (Ephesians 1:5, 6) And "we have obtained an inheritance, being predestinated according to the purpose of him who worketh all things after the counsel of his own will." (Ephesians 1:11) "For whom he did foreknow, he also did predestinate to be conformed to the image of his Son, that he might be the firstborn among many brethren. Moreover whom he did predestinate, them he also called: and whom he called, them he also justified: and whom he justified, them he also glorified." (Romans 8:29, 30) Election is not something that is hid from us, but revealed as the eternal fountain of all the blessings of salvation that are bestowed upon us in Jesus Christ our Lord.

But the text in Peter also speaks of the calling: "give diligence to make your calling and election sure." There can be no doubt that the calling unto salvation is meant. And that, too, is the work of God. It is that wonder of God's grace whereby the sinner, who is dead through trespasses and sins, who is without God in the world and stands in enmity against God, is translated from death unto life, from darkness into light, so that he hears the voice of the God of his salvation speaking to him through Christ Jesus, embraces Him as his Lord and Redeemer, and finds rest for his soul; and whereby, too, he leaves the way of sin and unrighteousness, repents, and has a new delight in the law and precepts of his God. Of this calling the apostle Peter had spoken in the beginning of this same chapter in which he admonishes us to make our calling and election sure, when he wrote: "According as his divine power hath given unto us all things that pertain unto life and godliness, through the knowledge of him that hath called us to glory and virtue: Whereby are given unto us exceeding great and precious promises: that by these ye might be partakers of the divine nature, having escaped the corruption that is in the world through lust." (vss. 3, 4)

We may notice that in the exhortation to make our calling and election sure the calling is mentioned first. The reason for this is not that actually the calling precedes election: for the very opposite is true. Election is the source of all our salvation, also of the calling: whom He hath predestinated, them He also called. (Romans 8:30) But the reason must be found in the fact that the apostle here admonishes believers to give diligence to make their calling and election sure. This cannot mean, of course, that our election and calling are not sure with God, and that it depends on us, on our faithfulness and perseverance, to make them sure. For the gifts and calling of God are without repentance. But it does mean that we must put forth effort to make them sure for our own consciousness, so that we are established in the faith and live and walk in the joyful assurance that we are children of God, that we are heirs of eternal life, that with body and soul, for time and eternity, we belong to our faithful Savior Jesus Christ, and that nothing can ever pluck us out of His hand, nor separate us from the love of God in Him. This is the reason, no doubt, why the apostle mentions the calling, and not election, first. It is, of course, quite impossible to make sure of our election first, and then of our calling.

For it is in the calling that we receive the fruit of election. In the calling the God of our salvation, Who ordained us unto glory, reaches down to save us and to give us eternal life in Christ. In the calling we experience our election. And therefore, we must give diligence to make our calling sure, and through that personal assurance of our calling reach out and lay hold by faith upon our own election from before the foundation of the world.

But some may, perhaps, ask: why should it be necessary to give diligence to make our calling and election sure? Does it require special effort to become sure of our eternal salvation? Does not a Christian know that he is saved, that God called him out of darkness into His marvelous light, and is he, therefore, not spontaneously sure of his calling and election? Does he not believe in Christ, and is not his salvation a matter of his experience? Why then should he give diligence? Why should he put forth special effort to make his calling and election sure?

However, the matter of our own salvation and of the assurance of our calling and election is not quite so simple. We should not speak and assume the attitude as if it were quite natural for the believer that he always live on the mountain tops of faith and in the bright and glorious sunshine of the full assurance of eternal glory. For to speak thus would be to ignore utterly the reality and actual position of the Christian in this world, and it would be contrary to the experience of every true believer. We must not forget that we are still in this world, not yet in heavenly perfection, and that in this world there are many forces that oppose our faith and that combine to deprive us of the assurance of our calling and election. First of all, salvation is heavenly, and we are earthly. Salvation belongs to the things which eye hath not seen, and ear hath not heard, and have never arisen in the heart of man. And the things that are seen engulf us on every side, have a strong hold on us, tempt us to seek the things that are below, rather than the things that are in heaven. Secondly, we lie in the midst of death, even though we have eternal life in us through Jesus Christ. We suffer and die as all men. How easy it would seem for that power of death, which is after all God's own hand, to persuade us that God is still against us, and that we are not His children! And then, there is our old nature, and there are the motions of sin in our members, and there is the world in the midst of which we live, tempting us from the way of righteousness. What Christian does not know by experience how his own sin can rise up against him, and for a time cast a dark shadow of fear and doubt over his soul? Mark you well, I do not say that it is right for the believer to live in doubt and fear as to his calling and election. But I do say that there is plenty of reason for the Christian in this world to heed the exhortation, "Give diligence to make your calling and election sure!"

But the question arises: how can this be done? What must we do to make our calling and election sure?

In the light of this exhortation we dare not, of course, assume the attitude that it is impossible for the believer in this life to be sure of his personal salvation and to live in that glad assurance. One meets with Christians occasionally who assume this stand. One can never be sure, say they, of his calling and election until he finally is glorified with Christ in heaven. The best we can do is doubt and hope for the best. But this would be disobedience to the Word of God in our text, which exhorts us to give diligence to attain to this assurance. Nor must we hope for and expect some sort of special revelation from God assuring us that He wrote our name in the book of life from before the foundation of the world. Such a hope would not only be vain because it will never be realized; but it would also be detrimental for our spiritual life. For if thus, by a special voice or vision from heaven, God would assure us of our eternal election and salvation, we would rest on this revelation and give no more diligence to make our calling and election sure. And the text evidently would have us put forth effort, give special diligence, in order to live and walk in the assurance of our calling and election. For the same reason one cannot appeal to certain mystical experiences, feelings, whisperings of the Spirit, or the like, for this assurance. Nor, finally, must he try to base his assurance of salvation on his conversion in the past. Many seem to make this attempt. They were converted several years ago, and they know it. They accepted Christ as their personal Savior there and then. And because they vividly remember this conversion of years ago, they know that they are saved today. But also this is contrary to the text, which does not tell us to appeal to some past experience, but to give diligence today and tomorrow, every moment of our life, to make our calling and election sure.

How, then, does one obtain this assurance of election and calling? I would answer this question as follows. First of all, it must be emphasized that also this assurance is a gift of grace and that it can rest only on the Word of God addressed to us. Only God can assure us of our salvation. On nothing less dare we base our assurance. But how does God speak to us? Always through the Scriptures. Apart from the Word of the gospel there is no Word of God to us. Hence, if we would make our calling and election sure, we must surely give diligence to read and study the Scriptures and to attend to the Word of God preached. But how do we know that God speaks to us personally? The answer is: He speaks to us by His Spirit, and thus applies the Word of the gospel to us personally, calling us evermore out of darkness to His marvelous light, and witnessing with our spirit that we are the sons of God. (Romans 8:16) But here we must remember that this testimony of the Spirit that we are the sons of God is heard by us through the gospel only in the way of sanctification, the way of God's precepts, the way of repentance and conversion, the way in which the Spirit leads. In the way of sin and corruption, the way of the world and of the flesh, the Spirit does not witness with our spirit that we are children of God.

On the contrary, in that way we grieve the Spirit; and we receive the testimony that we are still in our sins. If, then, we would make our calling and election sure, we must give diligence to walk in the way of light and righteousness, to fight the good fight of faith, according to the calling wherewith we are called.

It is especially this element which the apostle Peter has in mind when he exhorts believers to make their calling and election sure. For in the context he admonished them to add on their part all diligence that they might supply virtue in their faith, knowledge in virtue, self-control in their knowledge, patience in their self-control, godliness in their patience, brotherly kindness in their godliness, and love in their brotherly kindness. Giving diligence, then, to walk in that Christian way of faith and knowledge, of patience and godliness, of brotherly kindness and love, walking in the light with all the saints, and that, too, in the midst of a world that lieth in darkness, we shall hear the Word of God, through the Scriptures, by the Spirit, assuring us of the grace of our personal calling and election.

It is evident that this task is never finished, as long as we are in this life. One can never say: I made my calling and election sure long ago, and now I need give no more attention to that. On the contrary, the exhortation is for all of us, for every believer; and daily he must heed it. Every day he has need to live close to the Word of God in the Scriptures, to fight the battle of faith, that he may walk as a child of light in the midst of a world of sin, in order that in that way he may be conscious of the testimony of God's Spirit assuring him of his personal salvation. Only in that way, but in that way surely, can he walk in the glad assurance that he is Christ's, and that nothing can ever separate him from the love of God!

Chapter 15

GLORIFIED THROUGH GRACE

> ... and whom he justified, them
> he also glorified.
>
> — Romans 8:30

The believer in this world *is* saved. For the apostle writes, not that we shall be, but that we are saved by grace, through faith. (Ephesians 2:8) He that believeth on the Son *hath* everlasting life. (John 3:36) And the Lord solemnly declares: "Verily, verily I say unto you, He that heareth my words, and believeth on him that sent me, hath everlasting life, and shall not come into condemnation; but is passed from death unto life." (John 5:24) For such a one the hour has come "when the dead shall hear the voice of the Son of God: and they that hear shall live." (John 5:25) He is under grace, and therefore sin no longer has dominion over him. (Romans 6:14) There is no condemnation for him, and the law of the Spirit of life in Christ Jesus hath made him free from the law of sin and death. (Romans 8:1, 2) As a son of God, he is led by God's Spirit, the Spirit of adoption, Who also witnesses with his spirit concerning his sonship, and whereby he cries: Abba, Father! (Romans 8:14-16) In fact, he is raised with Christ and made to sit together with all the saints in heavenly places in Christ Jesus. (Ephesians 2:6) The believer is regenerated, called, justified, and sanctified, begotten unto a lively hope through the resurrection of Jesus Christ from the dead. Salvation is not only a future hope; it is also a present reality.

Yet, although all this is true in principle, the goal has not yet been attained. Final perfection still seems far off, and the Christian has his eyes expectantly turned toward the future for the full realization of salvation in Christ which he now possesses in principle. "Beloved, now are we the sons of God, and it doth not yet appear what we shall be: but we know that, when he shall appear, we shall be like him; for we shall see him as he is." (I John 3:2) Together with all creation we also, "which have the firstfruits of the Spirit, even we ourselves groan within ourselves, waiting for the adoption, to wit, the redemption of our body." (Romans 8:23) And "we that are in this tabernacle do groan, being burdened: not for that we would be unclothed, but clothed upon, that mortality might be swallowed up of life." (II Corinthians 5:4) We are saved; yet it seems a far cry from our present state to final glory. We are redeemed, we are justified; yet our conscience accuses us that we still sin daily against all the commandments of God, and the goal of our salvation is not reached until that conscience can find no more occasion to accuse us. We are delivered from the bondage of sin, holy in Christ Jesus; yet we know but too well that in us, that is, in our flesh, dwelleth no good thing; and we are not fully saved until we shall be delivered from the body of this death. We are children of God, yet we must wait for our final and public adoption; heirs of God in Christ, yet we possess nothing; victorious, yet here in the world we suffer defeat outwardly. We are alive in Christ, yet we die as all other men and seem to be of all men most miserable. We are citizens of the heavenly commonwealth, yet we are in the earth as sojourners and strangers. We are alive in the midst of death, righteous in the midst of sin, holy in the midst of corruption, blessed in the midst of misery, immortal and yet mortal, heavenly and yet earthly, saved indeed and yet looking for salvation. We must be glorified!

On this final salvation the Scriptures throughout fix the hopeful gaze of the children of God. In the midst of trouble the psalmist is inspired to sing: "Thou shalt guide me with thy counsel, and afterward receive me to glory." (Psalm 73:24) His heart is glad, and his glory rejoiceth, and his flesh shall rest in hope: for he knows that his God will not leave his soul in hell nor suffer His holy one to see corruption. Through the midst of death Jehovah will show him the pathway of life, leading him into His very presence, where there is fulness of joy and in Whose right hand there are pleasures for evermore. (Psalm 16:9-11) The Lord will surely give to Zion "beauty for ashes, the oil of joy for mourning, the garment of praise for the spirit of heaviness; that they might be called trees of righteousness, the planting of the Lord, that he

might be glorified." (Isaiah 61:3) And He will create "new heavens and
a new earth: and the former shall not be remembered, nor come into
mind." (Isaiah 65:17)   The Lord comforts the troubled hearts of His
disciples with the prospect of His Father's house in which there are
many mansions, and in which He prepares a place for them, in order
that they may be forever where He is. (John 14:1-3) The apostle Paul
writes that "we rejoice in hope of the glory of God" (Romans 5:2); and
that "the sufferings of this present time are not worthy to be compared
with the glory which shall be revealed in us." (Romans 8:18) It is a
glory in which the whole creation shall participate: "For the earnest
expectation of the creature waiteth for the manifestation of the sons of
God."   For the creature is, indeed, in bondage of corruption, subject
to vanity; but it is such in hope: for it shall be delivered from that
bondage into the glorious liberty of the children of God. (Romans
8:19-22) And "we know that if our earthly house of this tabernacle
were dissolved, we have a building of God, an house not made with
hands, eternal in the heavens." (II Corinthians 5:1) Moreover, we are
assured that the last enemy, that is, death, shall be destroyed, that we
shall be raised incorruptible, and that the saying shall be accomplished,
"Death is swallowed up in victory." (I Corinthians 15:26ff.) We are
"begotten again unto a lively hope by the resurrection of Jesus Christ
from the dead, to an inheritance incorruptible, and undefiled, and that
fadeth not away." (I Peter 1:3, 4) And in the last chapters of the Book
of Revelation a glorious picture is held before us of the New Jerusalem
in the new creation, in which the tabernacle of God shall be with men,
"and he will dwell with them, and they shall be his people, and God
himself shall be with them, and be their God. And God shall wipe away
all tears from their eyes; and there shall be no more death, neither
sorrow, nor crying, neither shall there be any more pain: for the
former things are passed away." (Revelation 21:3, 4)

But what is the meaning of this state of glory for which we hope and
which is the ultimate realization of the wonder of God's grace in Christ
Jesus our Lord?

The heart and essence of it is, undoubtedly, perfect fellowship with
God as His friend-servants. To be received, according to the measure
and capacity of the creature, in God's own family, to live His own life,
to dwell in His house, to taste that He is good, to enter into His secrets,

to know Him even as we are known, to see Him face to face, to love Him and be loved of Him without fear, to walk with Him and talk with Him in most intimate communion, and then to consecrate ourselves and all things to Him as His servants, to have our delight in His perfect will, and to glorify Him for ever — that is the heart of the heavenly blessedness for which we look. Everywhere this receives the emphasis in Scripture. God is building a house in which we shall dwell with Him under one roof, as one family, as a company of friends; a tabernacle in which He shall dwell with us and be our God; the house of many mansions, a home in which He will be our Father and we shall be His sons and His daughters. (John 14:1-3; II Corinthians 6:16-18; Revelation 21:3) And then we shall truly know Him with the knowledge of perfect love: for "this is life eternal, that they might know thee the only true God, and Jesus Christ whom thou hast sent." (John 17:3) Now we know in part, but then we shall know even as we are known; now we see as in a glass darkly, but then we shall see face to face, and we shall see Him as He is. (I Corinthians 13:12; I John 3:2) Then shall be perfected what the Lord Jesus declared in His beautiful sacerdotal prayer: "I in them, and thou in me, that they may be made perfect in one." (John 17:23) And this fellowship of friendship, in which we shall serve God as His friends, will be raised to the highest possible degree of perfection in the sphere and on the plane of heavenly glory. It will not be a return to the original state of rectitude and bliss in the first paradise but will be exalted above that state as Christ is exalted above the first Adam. And it will be everlasting. No tempter shall be able to intrude into that house of God and to destroy that state of perfect blessedness; nor shall there be any possibility of falling into sin and death again. For that perfect glory is centered in the Son of God in our nature, our Lord Jesus Christ. Such is eternal life!

Unto that central idea of heavenly life with God all things shall be adapted. We ourselves shall be so changed that we will be able to inherit that kingdom and to live in that sphere of perfect fellowship with God. For we must all be changed. Flesh and blood cannot inherit the kingdom of God. (I Corinthians 15:50)

This change is threefold. First of all, we shall be made spiritually, ethically perfect: we shall be made like Him, that we may see Him as He is. Being made perfectly sinless, we shall stand in everlasting knowledge, righteousness, and holiness, without spot or wrinkle before His face. Secondly, we shall be made heavenly. All that is of the earth earthy shall be put away, and we shall be clothed with heavenly glory and endowed with heavenly powers. We shall be given heavenly eyes to see things heavenly, heavenly ears to hear things heavenly, clothed upon with heavenly glory to be able to dwell in God's heavenly tabernacle. For "The first man is of the earth, earthy: the second man is the Lord from heaven. As is the earthy, such are they also that are earthy: and as is the heavenly, such are they also that are heavenly. And as we have borne the image of the earthy, we shall also bear the image of the heavenly." (I Corinthians 15:47-49) Finally, we shall be clothed with immortality and incorruptibility, that death may forever be swallowed up of life, and that, too, in body and soul. "For this corruptible must put on incorruption, and this mortal must put on immortality. So when this corruptible shall have put on incorruption, and this mortal shall have put on immortality, then shall be brought to pass the saying that is written, Death is swallowed up in victory." (I Corinthians 15:53, 54) Thus perfected, transformed into the image of the heavenly, and clothed with immortality, we shall be able to inherit the kingdom of heaven and to dwell in God's heavenly tabernacle forever.

But also creation itself shall be adapted to be the stage of and to serve this perfected covenant of God, this life of heavenly friendship in the tabernacle of God. This present creation shall pass away, and there will be found no place for it anymore. (Revelation 20:11) "The heavens shall pass away with a great noise, and the elements shall melt with fervent heat, the earth also and the works that are therein shall be burned up." (II Peter 3:10) But they shall not be annihilated. The wonder of grace shall embrace all things and shall make all things new. For also the creature itself, which has been put under bondage, shall be made free, and shall become partaker of the glorious liberty of the children of God. For "we, according to his promise, look for new heavens and a new earth, wherein dwelleth righteousness." (II Peter 3:13) And John saw "a new heaven and a new earth: for the first heaven and the first earth were passed away; and there was no more sea." (Revelation 21:1) From that new heaven and earth death and hades shall forever be banished into the lake of fire; and it shall be one heavenly creation, earth and heaven united, with its center in the New

Jerusalem and its everlasting head in Christ, that God may be all in all. And in that new creation all things shall serve us, that we may serve our God!

You will readily understand that this transformation of ourselves and of all things can be accomplished only by the wonder of God's grace in Jesus Christ our Lord. Not by a process of gradual development can we be translated from our present state of earthly imperfection into the state of heavenly glory and perfection. Nor can our present universe by gradual development attain to the glory of the new heavens and the new earth. The first Adam could not possibly have developed into the second Adam. The sinner, dead and corrupt in sin and misery, cannot possibly be reformed into a living child of God. The first Adam must die, to make room for the second. Only the wonder of grace in regeneration can make us new creatures in Christ Jesus. The same is true of our glorification and of the liberation and regeneration of all things: we must be glorified by grace.

By this we mean not only that Christ has merited this glory for us and that, therefore, it is freely bestowed upon us, but also that it is by the marvelous power of grace that this transformation into heavenly glory will be realized. For in its widest and all-comprehensive sense, grace is that wonderful power whereby God in Christ raises us and the whole creation from the depth of sin and death and the curse to the height of everlasting and heavenly glory in Christ Jesus our Lord. That wonder of grace is centralized in the incarnation, God dwelling with us in the flesh of Jesus Christ. It is based upon the atoning death of our Lord: God was reconciling the world unto Himself in Him. It is centrally realized in the resurrection of Jesus Christ from the dead and in His exaltation at the right hand of God, whereby He has received power even to subdue all things under Himself. (Philippians 3:21) That wonder of grace is realized in us through the Spirit which He hath given us and through Whom we receive the beginning of salvation even now. By the wonder of grace we are regenerated, translated from death unto life. By the wonder of grace we are called, translated from darkness to light. By the wonder of grace we are justified, sanctified, and preserved even unto the end in the midst of this world of sin and death. But it is also by the wonder of grace that presently, when the earthly house of this tabernacle shall be dissolved, our spirit shall be glorified and perfected to be with Christ in God's house. It is by the wonder of grace that our bodies shall sleep in the dust of the earth till the day of the resurrection, and that in that day they shall be raised, so that this corruptible shall put on incorruption, this mortal shall put on immortality, and death shall be swallowed up in victory. By the wonder of grace the image of the earthy which we now bear shall be transformed into the image of the heavenly, that we may be like Christ. And, finally, by the power of that same wondrous grace the present creation shall pass through the final catastrophe, to come forth out of the world-fire purified and renewed, in heavenly beauty and glory, that all things in heaven and earth may be united in Christ forever, and God may be all in all.

And all this is done to the glory of that wonderful God, Whose delight it is to call the light out of darkness, righteousness out of sin, holiness out of corruption, life out of death, heavenly glory out of the desolation of hell! "O the depth of the riches both of the wisdom and knowledge of God: how unsearchable are his judgments, and his ways past finding out! . . . For of him, and through him, and to him, are all things: to whom be glory for ever. Amen."